Vittorio Serra

# Venice

## new practical guide

*167 color illustrations*
*Map of the city*
*Useful information*

BET
BONECHI EDIZIONI "IL TURISMO" FIRENZE

*Exclusive distributor for Venice*:
BENEDETTI SOUVENIRS S.a.s. di Roberto Benedetti & C.
Via Cannaregio 3548/49
30121 VENICE
Tel. (041) 71.87.82 - 72.09.77
Fax. (041) 52.40.767

© Copyright 1998 by Bonechi Edizioni "Il Turismo" S.r.l
Via dei Rustici, 5 - 50122 FLORENCE
Phone +39 (55) 239.82.24
Fax.+39 (55) 21.63.66
E-mail: barbara@bonechi.com
         bbonechi@dada.it
http://www.bonechi.com
Printed in Italy

*Photos*: The Bonechi Edizioni "Il Turismo" S.r.l.Archives
*Photos*: Paolo Bacherini
         I-Buga S.a.s. Milan: p. 2, 14 (above), 19 (above), 20 (above),
         94, 110 (below), 112 (below).
         Giorgio Deganello: interior of St. Mark's Basilica
         *The photographs of the works inside St. Mark's Basilica were*
         *made available through the courtesy of the Procuratoria di San*
         *Marco di Venezia.*
         Nicola Grifoni: p. 12, 22 (above), 28, 77 (above), 95, 104
         (above), 105, 107 (below).
*Translated by*: Julia Weiss
*Text revised by*: Studio Comunicare, Florence
*Cover design and layout*: Lorenzo Cerrina
*Photolithography by*: Bluprint S.r.l., Florence
*Printed by*:BO.BA.DO.MA., Florence
**ISBN 88-7204-332-8**

We wish to express our special thanks to the **Peggy Guggenheim Collection** for the text and photographs on pages 89, 90.

# VENICE «QUEEN OF THE ADRIATIC»

First of all, why Venice? Let us go back to the time when non-Italic Indo-Europeans settled in the Venetian plains. They very probably came from Illyria in the second millenium B.C. and over-ran the Euganean hills, founded Vicenza, Treviso, Padua, Este, Belluno and other centers. In the first century B.C., these towns were Romanized and it was at this point that the local population was given the name of Venetians. The word Venetians, if truly of Indo-European origin, could mean «noblemen»; if, on the other hand it is pre-Indo-European, its meaning would be «foreigners» or «newcomers». It is to be presumed, therefore that «newcomers» or «novi venti» led to Veneti (Venetians) and thence to Venezia (Venice).

Venice took many centuries to develop. The nucleus of the original settlement was in the area of today's Rialto district. A network of canals was planned and the earth the builders dug up, was used to strengthen the islands of the lagoon. The Grand Canal and the innumerable «rii» (lesser canals) of Venice, which by means of 400 bridges, link over 118 islets to each other today, came into being over the centuries: tree-trunks were tightly bound together and used to consolidate the muddy little islands, constituting the foundations of the houses and palaces. From East to West, the town measures 4,260 meters and from North to South it is 2,790 meters wide. It covers an area of 7,062 Kmsq. and its perimeter (including the islands of the «Stazione Marittima» (The Ferry Terminal), the island of St. George, of St. Helen and the island of Giudecca is 13,700 metres.

When Venice first appears, it looks like a dream-city, springing like a gleaming splendid vision from the waters of the lagoon. Its delicate beauty changes with the seasons and unfolds countless treasures: historical places, natural beauties, art, the traditional hospitality and kindness of the people all make it a truly unique place. The famous Grand Canal or «Canalazzo», as it is called by the Venetians, with its marvellous succession of beautiful «palazzi» and picturesque houses, is the main thoroughfare. Its inverted S winds for 3,800 metres through the town and at some points it is 30 and at others 70 meters wide; it is from 5 to 5 and a half meters deep. It flows from North-West to South-East (dividing Venice in two) into the much wider St. Mark's Canal, which reflects the sparkling bulk of the Ducal Palace. The Grand Canal, crossed by three bridges (the Railway bridge, the Rialto and the Academy bridges), together with the 45 «rii» (little canals) that flow into it, link all the «sestieri» (districts) of the town to each other. The typical «rii» or «rielli» are mostly about 4 or 5 meters wide and can only be used by gondolas. The «rii» are nearly always flanked by narrow, twisty pathways or alleys called «calli». The calli lead into little clearings or squares called «campi» - if fairly large, or «campielli» - if small. The «rii» can also lead into little dead-ends or courtyards, called «corti».

Venice is divided into six «sestieri»: St. Mark, Castello, Cannaregio, Santa Croce, St. Paul, and Dorsoduro (which includes the parish of St. Eufemia on the island of the Giudecca). There are about 100,000 people living in the «sestieri». Venice is 4 kms away from the mainland and is linked to it by ferry-boats, a double railway bridge (3,601 meters long and built 1841-46) and by a road bridge, built in 1931-32, which is 4,070 meters long and 20 meters wide. The two bridges run together for quite a long way.

## THE CLIMATE

Venice is fortunate in having a very temperate climate. As a matter of fact, the average yearly temperature is 14.4° centigrade; winter is rarely very cold and summer is not too hot; there is abundant rainfall from summer to autumn. The «grecale» hits the town in May, when this wind comes sweeping in from the Adriatic. The North-Easterly wind which hits the town in winter is sometimes called the «Bora». During the so-called high tide or «acqua alta» (high water), as the Venetians call it, the town takes on a very strange appearance. As a rule, the waters invade the Piazza San Marco, rising to about half a meter above the level of the square, so that the gondolas can come rowing right into the middle of it. The poor residents have to use improvised raised platforms and gangways to get around the flooded area. These periodic floods are one of the main causes of erosion in the foundations of the various public and private buildings of Venice.

## PATRON SAINT, PIGEONS AND GONDOLAS

Venice has had two Patron Saints: St. Todaro (Theodore), of

Greek origin, who embodied the feeling of allegiance tributed by the newly founded Republic to the Byzantine Empire, and St. Mark the Evangelist, whose body was brought to Venice in 828 by two Venetian merchants, who had removed it from the church dedicated to him in Alexandria in Egypt (where the saint had been martyred in the times of the Roman Emperor Nero) to save it from being desecrated by the Muslims. The holy relics were received with reverence and due honor was paid to them. The Saint was proclaimed Patron and protector of the town and as his symbol is a winged lion, the Lion of St. Mark became the town's emblem.

*The statue of the Doge Andrea Gritti before the Symbol of Venice,* by Ugo Botasso, detail of the western façade of the Doges' Palace.

Venice is also called «Serenissima» (most serene) because of the serene idea of justice which was the basis of all the social and political measures taken by the Government. The higher magistrates never belonged to any of the town's factions or political parties and were thus in a position to pass judgement on matters of public interest in a climate of aloof serenity. The Republic of Venice is thus nearly always represented allegorically holding the two symbols of Justice: the sword and the scales.

As soon as one arrives in Piazza San Marco, one is welcomed by festive clouds of pigeons. According to an old legend, the birds were first brought to Venice from Cyprus and presented to the wife of the Doge. For the Venetians the pigeons are the traditional ornament of the lovely square and are cared for by the Town Hall authorities, who see that they get a plentiful ration of corn every morning at nine plus another allowance at one P.M. During the tourist season, the pigeons receive supplementary rations from the innumerable visitors who hold out corn to feed them, in order to be photographed amidst a whirling cloud of fluttering wings.

But tourists are also fascinated by the gondolas that slide elegantly and silently along the waters of the Grand Canal or along one of the twisty «rii», evoking all kinds of romantic daydreams. As we are on the subject of gondolas, let us see where the word comes from. According to Mutinelli's «Lessico Veneto» (Venetian Lexicon), «gondola» comes from «cymbula» - a small boat.

The gondola is a small, asymmetrical, flat-bottomed rowing boat, generally possessing a single scull rowed from a standing position. The overall length is about four or five meters and the width about one meter fifty. The first gondolas appeared towards the end of the 13th century, but we do not know who invented them.

Touring Venice, we soon realize that the buildings can be grouped into four major categories of architectural styles. Each of them (Byzantine, Romanesque, Gothic and Renaissance) is typical of a period. Below we have briefly outlined their main characteristics.

## THE BYZANTINE STYLE

This style abounds in ornamentation, preci-

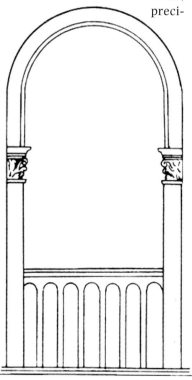

es. An essential feature of the Byzantine church are the columns, grouped to form galleries, that support the domes. The capitals, adorned with acanthus leaf and animal patterns, are usually topped with carved entablatures. The walls and ceilings are covered with rich mosaics. Although this style flourished mainly from the 6th to 12th centuries, it left its imprint on all periods of Venetian art.

## THE ROMANESQUE STYLE

This style spread all over Christendom during the early Middle Ages. It appeared in Venice as an offshoot of the Byzantine style towards the 11th-12th centuries. Romanesque churches are easily recognizable with their thick stone

ous materials, and dynamic forms, especially stressed by the use of arches and domes. The Byzantine dome is either sustained by four or eight columns (four if the shape is square, eight if it is octagonal) connected by arch-walls pierced by tiny windows. Inside, a double row of columns joined by round arches divides the nave from the aisles. The ceiling is often beamed.

## THE GOTHIC STYLE

The label "Gothic" dates from the Renaissance period, since the Italian Renaissance artists deemed Gothic art inferior to the purity of the art of Antiquity; for them "Gothic" was synonomous with barbarian (Goths). The style developed in Northern France in the 12th century. In Italy, and in particular in Venice, it flourished from the 12th through 15th centuries. Its main features are pointed arches, soaring yet airy eleva-

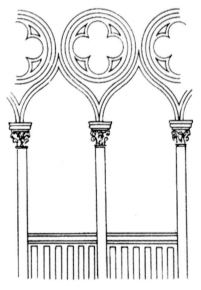

tions (in fact everything seems to be striving towards the sky), buttresses, and enormous windows divided into two or more zones by columns (the so-called mullioned windows) adorned with carved upper parts.

## THE RENAISSANCE STYLE

This is the style that, starting from the 15th century, signified the Italian artists' striving for a rebirth (rinascita) of the Antique, and, in fact, the Renaissance artists were inspired by Greek and Roman masterpieces which they adapted to the needs

and tastes of their own times. The main features of the Renaissance style are plain columns, round arches, use of friezes, cornices, trabeations and other Classical motifs, coffered ceilings either painted or carved, rectangular windows adorned with elaborate cornices resting on pilasters or columns, and richness of ornamentation. With the advent of the Baroque style in the 17th century, this richness becomes increasingly grandiose, until the straight line is almost completely supplanted by the curved line.

*View of the Grand Canal.* Opposite page: *the Fondaco dei Turchi.*

## ARRIVAL IN VENICE

Everyone who drives to Venice has to park in the **Piazzale Roma**, which is the huge parking lot and bus terminal for the buses linking the city to the mainland towns. The Piazzale is connected to the mainland by the **Ponte della Libertà** erected in 1933 alongside the 1876 railway bridge.

The building of the bridge and Piazzale was made necessary by the impelling need to facilitate both cargo and tourist connections with the mainland. Turning our backs on Piazzale Roma, we are now ready to enter the heart of the city by way of its main "thoroughfare," the **Grand Canal**. The most widely-used means of getting around in Venice is the vaporetto (water bus). Vaporetto service along the Grand Canal dates back to 1881. Proceeding along the **Rio Nuovo** and the **Papadopoli Gardens** we reach the **Pontile di Santa Chiara** (embarking station) on the **Fondamenta Santa Chiara** where we take a vaporetto for a scenic ride along the Grand Canal.

# THE GRAND CANAL

The Grand Canal, shaped like a huge upside down "S" bisecting the city, is almost 2½miles long, 15 feet deep, and ranges from about 100 to 225 feet across. Its aqueous "paving" sparkles in the sunlight, although the water is sometimes wave-capped and can even become sombre and menacing, depending on the weather and the season. Flanking the canal on either side is a parade of incredible buildings, brightly colored little houses alongside imposing stone palaces, dating from every period and exemplifying every architectural style. Even the most distracted sightseer cannot help but be enthralled by the vision of charming buildings, squares, tiny canals extending into the shadows, gardens stolen from the threatening grasp of the sea, and a lovely gateway here and there, blackened and corroded by the weather and the water. It is no wonder that painters and poets, musicians and writers have always expressed such great admiration for the canal. Byron, Canova, Wagner, Hemingway, among hundreds of others, all spent lengthy periods of their lives on or near its banks.

Immediately to our left we note the **Santa Lucia Station**. The railway station was named after the Palladian church dedicated to St. Lucy originally on the site, which was torn down in the middle of the 19th century to make way for the railroad linking Venice to the mainland. The railway bridge, officially inaugurated in 1846 was quite an engineering feat itself: 225 spans are supported by 75,00 pylons anchored in the depths of the lagoon. On the other hand, the station is actually a recent construction opened to the public in 1954.

From the station, proceeding in the direction of St. Mark's, we immediately note the attractive church of **San Simeone Piccolo** (also called San Simeone e Giuda) just to right of the station building. The most striking part of the church is its huge copper dome and lantern, surmounted by a statue of Christ the Redeemer, whose distinctive green color is due to the effects of weathering. The church dominates the whole first stretch of the Grand Canal, with its impressive staircase leading down to the water. Framing the entrance is an 18th century neo-Classical porch with Corinthian columns, designed by Giovanni Scalfarotto. The majestic gable crowning it is adorned with *Scenes of the Martyrdom of Saints Simeon and Judas* sculpted by Francesco Penso.

The first bridge we encounter on our way to St. Mark's is the **Ponte degli Scalzi**, also known as the Station Bridge. Made entirely

of white Istrian stone, it was designed by Eugenio Miozzi and put up in 1934 to replace a metal structure built in 1858 by the Lombard-Venetian city administration. The single span bridge is approximately 130 feet long and rises approximately 23 feet above water level. On the left bank by the bridge we note the imposing Baroque façade of the church of **Santa Maria di Nazareth** (or Santa Maria degli Scalzi).

Keeping our eyes riveted to the left side, our gaze encounters the apse and belfry of the church of **San Geremia** which was first built in the 13th century and later remodeled in 1760. Its Romanesque bell-tower dates back to the 13th century and is thus one of the oldest in the city. Alongside the church is a grandiose 18th century patrician palace, the **Palazzo Labia** whose interior was frescoed by Tiepolo. On the far corner is a statue of *St. John Nepomucenus* commissioned by one of the ladies of the Labia family. Still keeping our eyes to the left, just beyond the statue of the saint we see the beginning of the **Cannaregio Canal**, the second largest in Venice after the Grand Canal. Further on, this time on the right, is one of the most celebrated buildings in the Venetian Byzantine style, the **Fondaco dei Turchi**. The building was totally (and very arbitrarily) remodeled in the 19th century on the site of the 12th-13th century palace which was once the headquarters and trade center of the Oriental merchants stationed in Venice. Today it is the **Museum of Natural History**.

Once we have passed the Rio della Maddalena we encounter on

the left **Palazzo Vendramin Calergi**, an outstanding example of Renaissance architecture. Begun by Coducci and completed by Lombardo in 1509, it was where Richard Wagner died on February 13, 1883. A series of fine palaces follows. The first is the 17th century **Palazzo Ruoda**, with its completely remodeled façade. Just beyond we note the 16th century **Palazzo Gussoni-Grimani della Vida** attributed to Sanmicheli. Originally a fresco by Tintoretto adorned its façade, but like all other outdoor murals in Venice, this one too, corroded by brine and weathering, has been lost to us. Next we see the **Palazzetto Da Lezze** with its tiny façade over-

Preceding page, from above: *Palazzo Barbarigo; Palazzo Belloni-Battagia.*
Above: *the Ca' Pesaro.*

grown with vines, the 17th century **Palazzo Boldù** with its rusticated stone ground-floor, and lastly the **Palazzo Contarini-Pisani**, 17th century as well, with its spacious portico on the canal side.

Opposite these buildings is the majestic **Ca' Pesaro** acclaimed as Baldassarre Longhena's masterpiece of privately-commissioned architecture, and built between 1679 and 1710. So great did the building costs seem at the time that the architect is said to have died from worrying about whether the project would ever be finished. The imposing façade rises upon a rusticated stone base surmounted by a double tier of windows set off by clusters of columns. The building today houses the **International Gallery of Modern Art** and the **Oriental Art Museum**. On the same side, right by the Ca' Pesaro, is the **Palazzo Corner della Regina**, a Classical style building designed by Domenico Rossi (1724) on the site of the pre-existing Palazzo

*The Ca' d'Oro.*
Opposite page,
above: *the Fabbriche Nuove di Rialto;*
below: *the Pescheria.*

Cornaro. Today it is the headquarters of a banking organization.

Continuing along the left, we soon reach the most celebrated of the many remarkable buildings lining the Grand Canal, the **Ca' d'Oro**. After having been remodeled time and time again (and not always wisely) and passed from owner to owner, it came into the possession of Baron Giorgio Franchetti who in 1916 donated the palace along with the art collection bearing his name to the Italian state. The façade, which today is white, was originally gilded and this gave it its name - Ca' d'Oro, in fact, means Golden House. Built around 1440 for a nobleman, Marino Contarini, in a style which combines Byzantine influence with the Gothic pointed arch motifs, it looks like charming lace embroidery rising out of the Grand Canal.

On the ground floor is a portico which, except for the central round arch, is composed of graceful pointed arches. The two upper floors have delicately pierced loggias. The righthand section of the façade is more compact with fewer empty spaces, but it is in no way less elegant than the left side. Surmounting the façade is a crown of finely wrought crenellation.

On the left is another palace, the **Palazzo Sagredo**, a late 14th century Gothic building, with an elaborate façade. Across the canal, we cannot help but notice a two storey brick structure jutting out a bit from the other buildings. This is the **Pescheria**, or Fish Market which was built in 1907 by Domenico Rupolo after a design by the painter Cesare Laurenti. It opens on the Grand Canal by means of a spacious portico of slightly-pointed arches resting on columns which support a slanting roof to form the huge open loggia. The building rises on the site of what has always been Venice's fish market.

On the opposite side of the canal once more, we can make out the **Palazzo Michiel dalle Colonne** with its distinctive ground floor colonnade. The denomination "of the Columns" is thought by some to derive from these very columns, whereas others believe it was added to the Michiel name because it was a member of the family who actually brought the columns standing on the Piazzetta di San Marco from the Orient. Immediately after the Pescheria, again on the right bank, extends the impressive façade of the **Fabbriche Nuove di Rialto**. The building was put up in 1552 by Jacopo Sansovino and occupied by public offices having to do with trade and commerce. A bit beyond the Fabbriche Nuove we are struck by the colorful bustle of the open air fruit and vegetable market. The building bordering the marketplace, known as the **Fabbriche Vecchie di Rialto** was erected by Scarpagnino in 1522 as the seat of the court house. Facing the two Fabbriche is the **Ca' Da Mosto**, one of the most picturesque in Venice, in Venetian Byzantine-style.

The Grand Canal now curves

right and we are left speechless by the sight which meets our eyes upon passing the curve: before us is the Ponte di Rialto, or Rialto Bridge, in all its splendor. (We shall soon discuss it in greater detail). First, let us stop an instant and take a look at the **Fondaco dei Tedeschi** (German Storehouse) to our left. The building we see today was built in 1505 over the site of a pre-existing structure destroyed in a fire. It was designed by Scarpagnino in the Renaissance style with a spacious round-arch portico on the ground floor and a border of white crenellation on top. Unfortunately, nothing remains of the frescoes by Giorgione and Titian that originally adorned the façade. To the right is the **Palazzo dei Camerlenghi**, which was originally the Treasury of the Republic of St. Mark and thus the city's financial center. The building was erected in the early 16th century by Guglielmo Bergamasco. And thus we have reached the bridge which is one of the most famous, if not the most famous, in the whole world, the Ponte di Rialto.

# THE RIALTO BRIDGE

This is one of the best places to view the Grand Canal in all its charm. The Rialto is the oldest of the three bridges spanning the canal. Originally made of wood, it caved in in 1440 and was rebuilt, again of wood, but this time with the addition of several shops along it. It had a special mechanism which allowed the middle section to be moved, whereby even the tallest masted ships could sail through. It was somewhat unstable, though, unknown in such illustrious company, was awarded the commission and designed the bridge which was not finished until 1592. The Rialto is a single span bridge whose span measures 90 feet (the narrowest crossing of the Grand Canal is here) and has a maximum height of 24 feet at the middle. The two ends rest upon 12,000 pylons sunk into the muddy depths. The twenty-four shops lining the bridge are separated by a double arcade from which you can walk out on the terraces and get a superb view along the Grand Canal.

Just beyond the Rialto Bridge,

*The Rialto Bridge seen from the Grand Canal.*

and thus in the 16th century it was decided to build a new bridge. A competition was called, drawing the participation of such well-known architects as Michelangelo, Palladio, and Sansovino, all of whom worked on the project for years. Antonio Da Ponte, a relative on the right, is the **Palazzo dei Dieci Savi**, an early 16th century Renaissance building designed by Scarpagnino.

Farther ahead on the left bank are the 13th century **Palazzo Loredan** and the 12th century **Palazzo Farsetti** (today the Venice

*Palazzo Loredan and Palazzo Farsetti.*

*Palazzo Grimani.*

*Palazzo Papadopoli.*

City Hall), typical examples of the Venetian Byzantine style. The upper floors and balconies date from a 16th century alteration. On the same side, just a bit ahead, is a remarkable 16th century Renaissance building, Sanmicheli's masterpiece the **Palazzo Grimani**.

Today, the three storey palace with its handsome arcading, is occupied by the Venice **Court of Appeals**. On the right bank is the **Palazzo Papadopoli**, a 16th century building designed by Giacomo dei Grigi in the Classical style.

Next comes a fine 15th century

*Palazzo Bernardo.*

*Ca' Foscari.*

Gothic palace, **Palazzo Bernardo**, in which the Duke of Milan, Francesco Sforza. resided for some time. Past the Rio San Polo on the right bank, is an impressive 15th century building, the **Palazzo Pisani** with an intricate decorative motif adorning the center windows. Proceeding on the right, is the **Palazzo Balbi**, also known as "Palazzo in volta de Canal" (Corner Palace, because of its corner location).

Here the Grand Canal swings leftward and, on the right, by the Rio **Ca' Foscari**, is a famous 15th century Gothic building, the Ca' Foscari. Commissioned by Doge Francesco Foscari who ruled the Republic for over thirty years, it is now the Economics and Business School of the University of Venice.

The façade of Ca' Foscari has been acclaimed as one of the finest and best-proportioned in all of Venice. On the ground floor, six plain arched windows flank the great portal, while the upper floors are adorned with beautiful carved loggias whose lacy designs become more intricate with each storey. A bit farther along the left bank rises the 18th century **Palazzo Grassi**, built in 1718 by Giorgio Massari for the Grassi family of Bologna, and now occupied by the **Costume Institute**. The Classical façade has a rusticated stone ground floor and plain windows set off by simple balconies running the length of the two upper floors.

Opposite Palazzo Grassi on the right bank is a beautiful example of Venetian Classical architecture, the **Palazzo Rezzonico**. The ground and second floors were designed by Baldassarre Longhena who actually started construction in 1660 on a commission from the Priuli-Bon family. The building then came into the ownership of the Rezzonico family, who commissioned Giorgio Massari, the same architect who worked on Palazzo Grassi to finish it, although it was

*Palazzo Grassi;*
below: *Palazzo Rezzonico.*

not fully completed until 1745. The façade has a rusticated stone ground floor, while the two upper stories are adorned with balconies and columns which set off the individual windows. Inside the palace is the **Museum of 18th Century Venice**.

A bit farther on to the right is the 15th century Gothic **Palazzo Loredan dell'Ambasciatore** with its handsome façade. Inside the niches on either side are 15th century Lombard sculptures. Facing Palazzo Loredan is another 15th century Gothic building, **Palazzo Falier**, characterized by loggias on either side. We have now reached the last of the three bridges spanning the Grand Canal, the **Ponte dell'Accademia**.

This bridge too has only a single span. Although it appears to be completely made of wood, its weight-bearing members are, for safety's sake, actually metal. Before 1930, a 19th century all metal bridge stood in its place, but it was torn down because it

clashed too much with the rest of the Grand Canal's harmonious style. Beyond the bridge on the left is a turn-of-the-19th century building, the **Palazzo Cavalli-Franchetti** whose façade was inspired by the Venetian Gothic style. On the opposite bank is another fine Gothic building, the **Palazzo Da Mula** which dates from the end of the 15th century.

Farther on, on the same side, is a palace set in a lovely green park, the **Palazzo Venier dei Leoni** which houses **Peggy Guggenheim's collection of modern art**. Facing it is the attractive **Casina delle Rose** (Rose House) in which two celebrated Italians, Canova, the 18th century sculptor, and D'Annunzio, the early 20th century writer, lived at various times. On the left is the headquarters of the local prefecture, **Palazzo Corner**, also known as **Ca' Granda** (Big House) whose impressive size undoubtedly brought about its nickname. Jacopo Corner commissioned the architect Jacopo Sansovino to build it in 1535. Three centuries later, it was occupied by the Austrian governor. Opposite the Ca' Granda is the **Palazzo Dario**, a Renaissance building erected by

Above: *the Accademia Bridge*; left: *Palazzo Venier dei Leoni*.
Opposite page, above: *the Punta della Dogana*; below: *Santa Maria della Salute*.

Pietro Lombardo in 1487, whose façade is adorned with multicolor decorative motifs and marble ornamentation. Proceeding on the left is the 15th century Venetian Gothic **Palazzo Contarini-Fasan**, which has been dubbed "Desdemona's House". On the right we are struck by the sight of the majestic church of **Santa Maria della Salute** looming before us. This magnificent building is the masterpiece of Baldassarre Lon-ghena, whose contribution to the appearance of the Grand Canal was considerable.

Beyond the church is the **Punta della Dogana** upon which stands a 17th century tower surmounted by a globe supposed to mean good luck. From the 15th century onwards, duty on goods arriving from overseas was exacted on this spot. We are now at the place where the Grand Canal empties into the huge stretch of waterfront by St. Mark's.

As soon as we get off our vaporetto at the **Pontile di San Marco**, we are standing before a Lombard-style building erected in the 15th century. In the past it was occupied first by the Magistrato della Farina (Flour

Magistrate) then by the Academy of Painters and Sculptors (from 1756 to 1807, when it was headed by G. B. Tiepolo), and it is now the headquarters of the Venice Port Authority. Inside is a hall with a ceiling fresco by Jacopo Guarana (1773) depicting the *Triumph of Art.*

Further on is the **Giardinetto del Palazzo Reale**, a park on the site of the building where wheat was stored. At the end of the garden is the imposing **Palazzo della Zecca** designed by Sansovino in 1535. The rusticated stone arcading, Doric below and Ionic above, conveys an effect of stateliness and power, as befits the Mint of the Republic of St. Mark. This is where the celebrated zecchini d'oro (gold coins) were minted, the counterpart of the equally-renowned gold florins of Florence. Both were widely circulated throughout Europe and in the Orient. In 1870 the Zecca was closed down and since 1905 the building has been home to the reading room of the Marciana Library.

*Aerial view of St. Mark's Square and the Doges' Palace.*

## PIAZZETTA DI SAN MARCO

The Piazzetta serves as the simple but elegant antechamber to the grandiose Piazza San Marco. Two of the city's foremost monuments face on to it: the Doges' Palace on the east and the Libreria Sansoviana on the west. Originally a market for foodstuffs occupied this area, but then in 1536 the reigning doge decreed that the space should be kept clear.

By the docks are two monolithic columns (one with the **Lion of St. Mark** and the other with a statue of **St. Theodore**), both brought to Venice from the Orient in 1125. The two columns were set up on this spot in 1172 by a certain Niccolò Starantonio who had previously built one of the earliest wooden Rialto Bridges. The statue of St. Theodore (Todaro, in dialect) the first patron saint of Venice, standing atop the column, is actually a collage of different parts from different places, whereas the bronze lion on the second column is believed to be of Eastern, some even claim Chinese, origin. The Piazzetta was also the scene of public executions and between these columns both humble citizens and high-ranking personages were dealt the death sentence. Two of them passed into history. One was Pietro Faziol, known as "Il Fornaretto" (the baker's boy) who was executed after being unjustly charged with having killed a nobleman. Since then two oil lamps have been kept burning in his memory on the façade of St. Mark's nearest the Piazzetta. The other was the Count of Carmagnola, charged with high treason and executed on the same spot.

## LIBRERIA SANSOVINIANA
### (LIBRARY OF ST. MARK)

The Library takes up the whole west side of the Piazzetta. Considered Sansovino's masterpiece, it was defined as "the most sumptuous ever built" by the architect Palladio, while the writer Pietro Aretino remarked that it "surpasses envy".

The construction of a library to house the fabulous collection of rare books donated to the city by Cardinal Bessarione (who had been granted asylum here) was resolved by the Senate of the Republic in 1536.

## ST. MARK'S SQUARE

San Marco is the Venetians' incredible open-air drawing room, unique in all the world. Throughout its long, long history it has been witness to an endless stream of human events involving people from every walk of life, from the humblest artisans to the highest-ranking authorities, all of whom had a hand in creating the precious, incomparable treasure that is Venice. Looking back on the square's origins, we shall leave the description to a long-ago chronicler, Giuseppe Tassini, whose knowledge of his native town was truly incredible. In his book entitled Curiosità Veneziane (Venetian Curiosities), he recounts, "In olden times the Piazza San Marco was truly rustic. It was dubbed «morso» (tough) perhaps because its terrain was harder and tougher than the surrounding area and «brolo» (garden) because it was grassy and bordered by trees. On the opposite banks of the Batario Canal which crossed it were the two little churches of San Teodoro and San Gemignano erected, as is well-known, by Narsete who vanquished the Goths with the aid of the Venetian navy".

When St. Mark's Basilica and the Doges' Palace were being built, and under the reign of Doge Sebastiano Ziani (1172-1178), the Batario was filled in and the lawn in front of the building ripped out to pave this huge space, just about as large as it is today. On either side, elegant houses with arcades running their length were erected. A number of them were taken over by the Procuratori di San Marco (magistrates) which led to their present name of Procuratie. In 1264 the square was repaved in bricks in a herringbone design. This was replaced in 1723 by a more modern paving of grey Euganean trachyte and white marble, designed by Andrea Tirali. The trapezoid shaped square now measures 569 feet in length, 266 feet on the church side, and 185 feet on the opposite side. St. Mark's is especially enchanting at dusk when the lights go on. Music from the outdoor cafes fill the arcades and open spaces inviting one to leisurely stroll about or just sit and enjoy the passing parade.

*St. Mark's Square.*

## THE
## CLOCK TOWER

Facing the church, the Clock tower is on your left. It was built by Mauro Coducci between 1496 and 1499. The wings were added during 1500-1506, supposedly after a design by Pietro Lombardo, and later raised by Giorgio Massari in 1755. Above the tower is an open terrace on which stands a bell with a figure on either side. The bell is sounded by the hammering of the two male figures that were cast in bronze by Ambrogio de la Anchore in 1497 and dubbed the Moors because of the dark coloring they have taken on as their metallic surfaces have weathered over the

almost five hundred years they have been striking the hours in Venice.

Beneath the terrace, is the *winged lion,* symbol of St. Mark the Evangelist and the city of Venice herself. Below the lion is a jutting semi-circular balcony with a niche in the middle and a door on either side. The niche contains a gilded copper statue of the *Virgin and Child* which has been attributed to the sculptor and goldsmith Alessandro Leopardi who was born sometime in the second half of the 15th century and died 1522-1523. Each year on the feast-day of the Ascension (which comes 40 days after Easter) and during the whole time of Ascension week festivities, at the striking of every hour, figures of the Three Magi preceded by an angel, go in and out the

*The Clock Tower.*

doors, pass in front of the Virgin, and bow before her. The huge clock below the balcony was created at the end of the 15th century by two craftsmen, Giampaolo and Giancarlo Ranieri from

*Detail of the Clock Tower.*

Parma. The clock also indicates the changing of the seasons, the movement of the sun, the hours, and the phases of the moon. It was restored in 1757 by Bartolomeo Ferracina.

## THE PROCURATIE VECCHIE NAPOLEONIC WING THE PROCURATIE NUOVE

Extending the length of the Clock tower side of the square is the building known as the **Procuratie Vecchie** which has fifty arches on the ground floor level and two upper floors of loggias. It was begun between the end of the 15th and first half of the 16th centuries by Mauro Coducci who designed the first floor. Following the fire of 1512, Bartolomeo and Guglielmo Grigi succeeded Coducci and added the second storey, although the building was completed by Sansovino. The name "Procuratie Vecchie" (Old Magistrature) was given to distinguish the building from the "Procuratie Nuove" (New Magistrature) whose design is in keeping with the earlier building, so that the square conveys an effect of stately harmony and balance. On the far side of the square, the site of San Gemignano, a very old church which Napoleon ordered torn down in 1807 so that a huge ballroom entered from the royal palace, Palazzo Reale, could go up in its place, is the Ala Nuovissima (Brand-new Wing) or the **Ala**

*The Procuratie Vecchie and the Napoleonic Wing,* home of the Correr Museum.

**Napoleonica** (Napoleonic Wing). It is a neo-Classical design by Giuseppe Soli, who repeated the double orders of the **Procuratie Nuove**, adding a frieze of statues of Roman emperors and mythological and allegorical scenes to the top level. On the south side of the square is the Procuratie Nuove. Influenced by the Classical style of Sansovino's Library, Vincenzo Scamozzi designed it in 1584 and supervised construction up to the tenth arch. The rest was continued by Baldassarre Longhena, who finished it in 1640. This building too was once the residence of the Procuratori di San Marco but when the Republic fell in 1797 it was turned into the royal palace. Today it is occupied by cultural institutes such as the Correr and Archeological Museums.

## THE ARCHEOLOGICAL MUSEUM

An important collection of Classical art is laid out in twenty rooms of the Procuratie Nuove. Begun by Cardinal Domenico Grimani in 1523 and bequeathed by him to the Republic, it is made up of marble and bronze archeological finds from Rome and Greece. It was further expanded by the cardinal's nephew Giovanni Grimani, Patriarch of Aquileia.

Only the highlights of the twenty rooms will be indicated. **Room 1** contains an extensive collection of Greek and Roman inscriptions, of special interest for scholars. **Room 2** has four showcases in which a practically complete collection of Roman coins is on display. **Room 3** offers some fine pieces of Greek sculpture including *Hecates* (3rd century B.C.), the *Sosandra Aphrodite* (15th century B.C.) and a *Torso of Apollo*. **Room 4** contains outstanding 5-4th century B.C. sculptures: the *Headless Athena*, the *Grimani Hera*, and, in the center, the *Persephone* which dates from the time of Phidias. **Room 5**: Greek and Roman statues: *Ares and Aphrodite, Hercules and the Bull, head of Athena*. **Room 6** contains Greek and Roman Classical works including *Dionysus and the Satyr* and the celebrated *Grimani Ara* (altar). **Room 7**, of special note are the *headless Aphrodite*, the *funerary stele of Lysandra* and the superb *Zulian cameo, depicting Jupiter*, from Ephesus. **Room 8** contains Hellenistic works such as the 3rd century B.C. *Ulysses*, a Roman copy of a Greek original. **Room 9** has a fine collection of Roman portraits ranging from the Republican period to the 3rd century A.D.; those of *Pompeus* and *Vitellius* are especially fine. **Room 10**, Roman portraits continued. **Room 11**, shows Greek and Roman reliefs. In the showcases are ivories and small bronzes. **Room 12**, statues of *Venus*. **Room 13**, *Mithras Sacrificing a Bull*. **Room 14**, a series of finely-crafted vases. **Room 15** contains a fascinating collection of Roman altars, reliefs, and plaques. **Room 16** has reelaborated pieces of Classical art. **Rooms 17 and 18** display the Egyptian sculpture and Greek reliefs originally in the Correr collection. **Room 19** contains a fine Roman sarcophagus and prehistoric artefacts, Greek bronzes and ceramics. **Room 20**, the Near East collection, has Egyptian mummies and statuettes, and Assyrian reliefs.

# THE CORRER MUSEUM

The Museo Civico Correr oc-cupies the so-called Napoleonic or "Nuovissima" wing (west side) and the Procuratie Nuove (south side). The entrance is from the arcade of the Napoleonic wing. The collection was begun in 1830 by a wealthy Venetian nobleman, Teodoro Correr, who bequeathed his fabulous art works to his native city. The museum remained in the Palazzo Correr on the Grand Canal until 1922 when it was moved to its present site. The collection was so big it had to be split up into different sections: one pertaining to 18th century Venice displayed in the Palazzo Rezzonico, archeology in another wing of the Procuratie Nuove (entered from the Piazzetta), and those we are about to see, again broken up into three departments: History, Paintings, and 19th Century Italian History ("Il Risorgimento").

## THE HISTORICAL SECTION

In the room leading to the Historical Section is a youthful masterpiece by Antonio Canova, a statue of *Dedalus and Icarus*; the neo-Classical decorative scene is by G. Borsato. The museum, thirty-three rooms in all, contains a vast array of objects and furnishings relating to the history of Venice's institutions, art, and social changes. Among the highlights: the *Lion of St. Mark*, flags and emblems of the Republic, portraits and emblems of doges, decrees issued by the doges, descriptions of magnificent public ceremonies, attire worn by doges and high-ranking public officials, relics of the conspiracy led by Bajamonte Tiepolo, superb collections of coins, documents, naval formations, relics of the celebrated Battle of Lepanto, nautical maps and instruments, portraits of the great Venetian explorers and navigators and the great map of their colonial conquests, as well as fascinating weapons, emblems, flags, scepters, and trophies.

## THE PAINTING GALLERY

This section consists of nineteen superbly decorated rooms on the third floor. For reasons of space we cannot list all the works on display; we shall mention just the highlights in each room. **ROOM 1**: the Venetian Byzantine school: in addition to some fine paintings, there is a stupendous 13th century hopechest known as the *Cassa di Beata Giuliana* which shows Blessed Giuliana with Sts. Biagio and Cataldo. **ROOM 2**: 14th century Venetian painting, features works by Paolo Veneziano. **ROOM 3**: contains works by Lorenzo

Veneziano. Of special note is the panel showing *Christ Giving the Keys of the Kingdom to St. Peter* which originally was part of an altarpiece. **ROOM 4**: the 14th century panel paintings of *Virtues* and the early 14th century statuette of *Doge Tommaso Mocenigo*, by Jacopo Dalle Masegne should not be overlooked. **ROOM 5**: Venetian High Gothic painting: of major interest are Stefano Veneziano's *Virgin Enthroned* and, in the middle, a 14th century painted *Crucifix*. **ROOM 6**: Venetian High Gothic painting continued: a fine *Virgin and Child* by Jacobello del Fiore, and altarpiece with *Scenes from the Life of St. Mamante*, by Francesco dei Franceschi, and a *Virgin and Child* by Michele Giambono. **ROOM 7**: Cosmè Tura: displayed are masterpieces by the 15th century painter from Ferrara whose distinctive tormented style produced such remarkable paintings as this *Pietà*. **ROOM 8**: the Ferrarese School: there are other fine works by Ferrarese artists, as well as two superb *Virgins* by Bartolomeo Vivarini. **ROOM 9**: contains several Venetian wood sculptures. **ROOM 10**: the Flemish School

Preceding page: *Portrait of Doge G. Mocenigo*, by G. Bellini. Left: *The Courtesans*, by V. Carpaccio.

paintings, including an *Adoration of the Magi* by Pieter Brueghel. ROOM 11: three extraordinary paintings are to be found here: Antonello da Messina's *Pietà* (second half of the 15th century), Hugo Van der Goes' *Crucifixion* and *Bouts' Virgin and Child*. ROOM 12: among the Flemish and German masters displayed are Cranach, Bruyn, and Civetta. ROOM 13: the Bellinis. This family of artists dominated the whole Venetian art world from the early 15th to the beginning of the 16th centuries. Among the masterpieces of two generations of Bellinis here are Jacopo's *Crucifixion*, Gentile's *Portrait of Doge Giovanni Mocenigo* and Giovanni's *Transfiguration, Virgin and Child*, *Pietà* and a small *Crucifixion*. ROOM 14: Alvise

Vivarini and his followers, featuring a superb *St. Anthony of Padua*. ROOM 15: Vittore Carpaccio's most famous painting, *the Courtesans*. ROOM 16: Carpaccio and followers of Bellini, including a fine *Portrait of a Youth with a Red Beret*. ROOM 17: noteworthy are a *Virgin and Child* by Lorenzo Lotto, a *Bust of a Youth* by Giovanni Dalmata, and a *Virgin and Child with Saints* by Boccaccino. ROOM 18: the "Madonneri" (Greco-Venetian painters of the 16th and 17th centuries). ROOM 19: a collection of 16th century ceramics of incredible beauty and workmanship. The *Servizio Correr*, a service of seventeen pieces decorated by Niccolò Pellipario c. 1525, is particularly noteworthy.

## THE RISORGIMENTO MUSEUM

This 20-room section is devoted to relics of the period during which the Italians were struggling to attain their national identity and unity. It was set up after Venice was annexed to the Italian state under a bequest made by Piero Marsich, one of the main figures in the heroic but unsuccessful fight against the Austrians in 1848-1849. The rooms illustrate the fall of the Republic of Venice after a millenium of independence, the period of Napoleonic occupation, the Austrian domination, the conspiracies, the defense and surrender of the city in 1849 and finally, the liberation from the Austrians. The exhibit includes flags, relics of the famous patriots (foremost of whom Daniele Manin), weapons, oils and watercolors, as well as documents and photos, all related to the events of the Italian unity movement.

## THE BELL TOWER

*The Bell Tower of St. Mark's.*

This is the oldest bell tower in Venice, having been built over Roman foundations, starting from the time of Doge Pietro Tribuno (888-912) and then off and on over the years. Among the numerous artists who had a hand in it were Niccolo Barattieri and Bartolomeo Malfatto (the bell chamber), Proto Bon and Giorgio Spavento. For centuries it withstood the onslaught of storms and earthquakes. Then, at 10 a.m. on July 14, 1902, weakened by centuries of vicissitudes and less than perfect workmanship, it suddenly collapsed, luckily without causing a single victim or damage to the nearby monuments (except for Sansovino's Loggetta which was shattered into fragments and buried beneath the rubble). The loggia was put back piece by piece and the bell tower itself was reconstructed exactly as it had been on the same spot. It was re-opened to the public on the feast-day of St. Mark, the patron saint of the city, in 1912. All of Venice joined in the celebrations to welcome back the "paron de casa" (master of the house) as the Venetians dubbed the building whose bell chamber commands a remarkable view over the whole city and the lagoon. A convenient elevator will take you up to the bell chamber of the 320-foot tower. On top of the cusp is a gilded *angel* weathervane. When the tower collapsed in 1902, four of its five bells, the Angel, and the nearby Loggetta were all smashed to pieces, but they were put back together again with the painstaking labor of a Venetian craftsman, Emanuele Munaretti.

## THE LOGGETTA

At the foot of the Bell tower is the marvelous three-arched loggetta built by Sansovino between 1537 and 1549 to replace a 13th century one which, moved from the neighborhood of San Basso, had been erected here. In 1569 it housed the Armed Guard of the Republic when the Greater Council was in session. The four bronze statues in the niches of the facade depict *Apollo, Mercury, Pax* (Peace) and *Minerva* each symbolizing an aspect of the Republic: Apollo, its power; Mercury, the eloquence of its ambassadors and intellectuals; Peace, supposed to inspire the Venetians' political activities; and Minerva, the high level attained in the arts, sciences, government and war. The four statues are proof of the great skill that their creator, Sansovino himself, had achieved as sculptor in his mature period. The fine bronze gateway and putti on either side of the top are by Antonio Gai (1735). The allegorical reliefs (alluding to Venetian power) have been ascribed to Tiziano Minio and Danese Cattaneo.

## ST. MARK'S BASILICA

 The cathedral of Venice went up along with the Republic's rise as a sea power. In the year 828 the mortal remains of St. Mark the Evangelist were triumphantly borne to Venice and safety, far from the desecration supposedly in store from the Moslems of Alexandria of Egypt. Welcomed with solemn ceremonies and rites, the relics were at first placed in the Palatium Chapel, actually the tiny Church of San Teodoro. But it was hardly worthy of the new - and now sole - patron saint of the Serenissima Repubblica, so Doge Giustiniano Partecipazio decided to remedy the situation by bequeathing a considerable sum of money for the building of a basilica befitting such valuable relics. His wish was carried out by his brother, Giovanni Partecipazio, who set about the huge task of erecting a church alongside the Doges' Palace in 829. By 832 the building had all its main structures up and by 883 it was fully decorated. In 976, during an uprising of the Venetians against the despotic doge, Pietro Candiano IV, the Doges' Palace was set on fire and the flames also dam-

aged the adjoining basilica, which was only restored years later by the canonized doge, Pietro Orseolo. Then, shortly after the year 1000, Doge Domenico Contarini decided that the basilica was not equal to the magnificent churches being built in all the mainland cities and had it demolished. In its place he commissioned the church as we know it today. know it today. Building may have started as early as 1063 and was in any case terminated in 1073. The plan picked by the doge was wholly Byzantine, a Greek cross shape covered by a series of domes (although the treatment was more Romanesque than Byzantine), yet the name of the architect has not come down to us. Originally rather plain, if not austere-looking, St. Mark's was soon adorned with superb mosaics, precious marble from Roman Altinum, and various architectural and decorative elements from the Orient. For centuries, Venetian travelers, merchants, and admirals carted off war spoils and souvenirs to donate to the great church, so that today St. Mark's is a complex yet harmonious combination of Byzantine, Gothic, Islamic and Renaissance elements.

## THE FAÇADE

Along its approximately 169 feet runs a porch of five rounded arches protruding into the square. A delicate marble railing separates the ground floor level from the upper one with the four famous gilded bronze *horses*. The whole

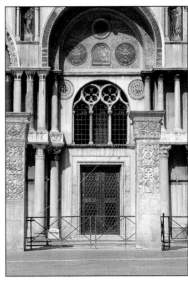

Preceding page: *the façade of St. Mark's Basilica.*
Above, left to right: *the Tetrarchs and the Pillars from Acre.*

building, dominated by five Oriental domes, seems unreal, almost as if it were a stage set. Before taking a more detailed look at the façade, we shall stop to observe the south side of the façade (i.e., that closest to the Doges' Palace). On the corner is a porphyry sculptural group showing two pairs of embracing male figures. The famous sculpture called "*the Tetrarchs*" is thought to be Syrian and most likely represents four emperors, namely Diocletian, Massimian, Galerius, and Constans. Nearby are two *square columns* which were brought here from St. John d'Acre in Syria. On the upper section of the church is a Byzantine mosaic depicting the *Virgin*. One of the perpetually-lit lamps near it recalls the legend of the poor baker's boy unjustly executed for a crime he never committed.

On the corner bordering the square is a truncated column, the "*pietra del bando*" (decree stone), which came from Syria. Here all the laws passed by the government were read aloud to the people assembled below.

We shall now take a closer look at the five portals opening into the square (starting from the right). In the first one bearing elaborate Moorish decorative motifs is a mosaic showing the *Removal of St. Mark's Body from Alexandria in Egypt*, a 17th century work by Pietro Vecchia. In the second one is another mosaic by Vecchia of the *Arrival of St. Mark's Body in Venice*. The central one is adorned with fine Venetian Romanesque bas-reliefs depicting *Professions*, *Months* and *Virtues*. Above the portal is a fine 12th century Romanesque sculpture of

Top to bottom:
*The Removal of St. Mark's Body from Alexandria;*
*The Arrival of St. Mark's Body in Venice;*
*The Venetians Venerating the Body of St. Mark;*
*Venetians Carrying the Body of St. Mark into the Church,* mosaic in the Portal of Sant'Alipio.

Facing page, top to bottom:
*The Deposition from the Cross;*
*Descent into Limbo;*
*Resurrection;*
*Ascension.*

the *Angel Appearing to St. Mark*. The mosaic above, representing the *Last Judgement* is a 19th century work after a design by Lattanzio Querena.

The fourth portal has a bronze door cast in the 14th century by Master Bertuccio. Above is a mosaic of the *Body of St Mark Being Venerated by the Venetians*, by Sebastiano Ricci (1728). The

fifth portal is called the Portal of Sant'Alipio after the statue of the saint to be found here. It is adorned with columns, capitals, and reliefs of various origins, mainly Byzantine, removed from older church buildings. The mosaic, datable 1260-1270, and showing the *Venetians Carrying the Body of St Mark into the Church* is especially fascinating

because it allows us to see what St. Mark's looked like at the time.

If you want a closer look at the works on the upper floor of the façade, you are allowed to walk out on the terrace from the galleries inside the church. However, to get a proper overall view of the façade, we recommend taking time out to walk far back on the square to embrace

the whole with a single glance. Beneath the elegant marble terracing between the arches are noteworthy 12th century Byzantine reliefs. From left to right, they portray: *Hercules and the Wild Boar*, the *Virgin*, *St. George*, *St. Demetrius*, *the Archangel Gabriel* and *Hercules and the She-Deer*. On the loggia above the main portal are the four marvelous 4th century B.C. Greek *horses* that Enrico Dandolo brought to Venice from Constantinople in 1204. They were on this spot from about 1250 until 1798 when Napoleon carted them off to Paris (they were returned to Venice in 1815). The horses were removed twice for safekeeping during both world wars. Behind the horses are four 11th century eight-sided columns with fine carved capitals and the huge window of the central arch. The mosaics in the smaller arches on either side, based on cartoons by Maffeo da Verona, portray (from left to right): the *Deposition*, the *Descent into Limbo*, the *Resurrection*, and the *Ascension*.

The elaborate decoration of the upper floor is one of the most remarkable sculptural compositions to have come out of Italian Gothic. Art historians believe that the project was begun by the Dalle Masegne family in 1385. Then, after a great fire in 1419 it was restored, continued, and altered by various Florentine and Lombard artists.

## LEFT SIDE OF ST. MARK'S, THE PIAZZETTA DEI LEONCINI, AND THE PORTA DEI FIORI

On the north side of the church is the Piazzetta dei Leoncini (literally, Square of the Lions) named after the two marble lions sculpted by Giovanni Bonazza in 1722. Before the Porta dei Fiori (Flower Portal) are three arches surmounted by fine Gothic sculptures. In the center of the first arch is a symbolic representation of the 12 *Apostles* (12 lambs). Then, after a relief of *Alexander the Great Carried up to Heaven*, a 10th century work, between the first and second arches, we find ourselves before the **Porta dei Fiori**. Unfortunately, nothing remains of the original construction, probably datable around 1200, the period when this side of the church was being remodeled. The Arab-Moorish style arch which has elaborate carvings of flowers and branches (and a lunette relief of a *Nativity*) gave the portal its name. After the fourth arch are five 12th and 13th centu-

*The Piazzetta dei Leoncini.* Opposite page: *the atrium of the Basilica.*

ry Byzantine reliefs. The finest shows *Christ Blessing the Four Evangelists*. Farther on, beneath an arch, is the *tomb of Daniele Manin* by Luigi Borro. Facing the Piazzetta is the Baroque façade of the suppressed **church of San Basso**, attributed to Giuseppe Benoni, and built c. 1670. In the center are marble fountains in the form of well-curbs and on the far side is the **Palazzo Patriarcale** with a neo-Classical façade by Lorenzo Santi (1837-1850).

## THE ATRIUM OF ST. MARK'S

In order to get the best possible view of the atrium, enter through the main portal. All aglow with a splendid mantle of golden mosaic, the atrium space is divided, by slightly pointed arches, into separate bays closed off by hemispherical domes, except for the central one (by the portal through which we entered) which is open. Measuring 201 x 19 feet and

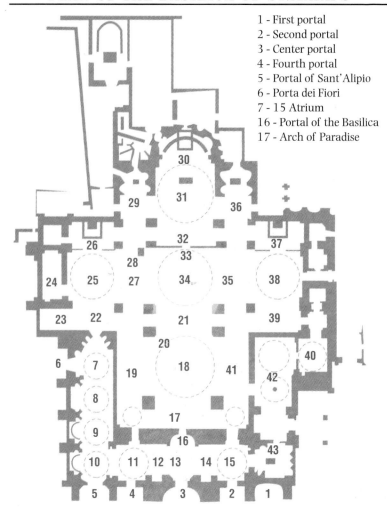

1 - First portal
2 - Second portal
3 - Center portal
4 - Fourth portal
5 - Portal of Sant'Alipio
6 - Porta dei Fiori
7 - 15 Atrium
16 - Portal of the Basilica
17 - Arch of Paradise

18 - Dome of the Pentecost
19 - Left nave
20 - Capital of the Crucifix
21 - West Arch
22 - Door of the Virgin
23 - Chapel of the Màscoli
24 - Chapel of Saint Isidore
25 - Chapel of Saint John
26 - Chapel of the Madonna Nicopeia
27 - North Arch
28 - Crypt of Saint Mark
29 - Chapel of Saint Peter
30 - Apse

31 - Main Altar
32 - East arch
33 - Ambos
34 - Dome of the Ascension
35 - South Arch
36 - Chapel of Saint Clement
37 - Altar of the Blessed Sacrament
38 - Dome of Saint Leonard
39 - Right Transept
40 - Treasure
41 - Right nave
42 - Baptistry
43 - Zen chapel

almost 24 feet tall, the atrium has remained unchanged for seven hundred years. The pavement too is covered with mosaics that create incredible light effects when the church is flooded, as it often is, in fall and winter. The marble columns against the walls are of various origins, some are even said to have come from the Temple of Solomon in Jerusalem.

Following the numbers on the map is the best way to look at the porch mosaics which recount stories from the *Old and New Testaments*. Practically all the mosaics were executed by Venetian masters who demonstrated incredible technical skill in their treatment of color and form. Their lively narrative style is typical of the Romanesque period.

**7** - The Porta di San Giovanni is opposite the Porta dei Fiori. On the dome and lunette are Scenes from the *Life of Moses* and, in the spandrels, figures of *Solomon, David, Zechariah* and *Malachi*. Directly over the door is the *Virgin and Child Between Sts. John and Mark*.

**8** - The dome recess contains 17th century mosaics executed after designs by Pietro Vecchio showing *Sts. Apollinaire, Sigismund* and *St. Francis with the Stigmata*. Scenes from the *Life of Joseph* (13th century) cover the dome, with the four *Evangelists* in the spandrels.

**9** - The Scenes from the *Life of Joseph* are continued. The tomb in the exedra is that of *Doge Marino Morosini* who died in 1253.

**10** - The mosaic in the semi-dome, executed in 1583 by Giuseppe Bianchini after a cartoon by Salviati, shows the *Judgment of Solomon*. The dome has Scenes from the *Life of Joseph*, with four *Hebrew Prophets* in the spandrels. All of these mosaics were done in 1240, but they underwent extensive restoration in the 19th century. An anonymous Pisan sculptor carved the *tomb of Doge Bartolomeo Gradenigo,* who died in 1342, which is visible in the exedra.

**11** - The lunette of the Porta di San Pietro has a Byzantine mosaic of *St. Peter*. The dome and side lunette contain several Scenes from the *Life of Abraham* in the Romanesque-Byzantine style.

**12** - The 13th century ceiling mosaic shows the *Drunkenness and Death of Noah*, the *Construction of the Tower of Babel*, and the *Weeping and Wailing of the Multitude*. The sepulchral wall contains *the tomb of Felicita Michiel*, wife of Doge Vitale Falier, who died in 1101.

**13** - In the upper niches is a *Virgin with Saints*; in the lower ones, *Apostles*. These works were done in the 12th century and were influenced by the Ravennate school. The bronze panel on the portal has figures of *Saints* cast between 1112 and 1138. The mosaic in the semi-dome, by Valerio and Francesco Zuccato who executed it in 1545 after a design by Titian, depicts *St. Mark in Ecstasy*. The same craftsmen also carried out the ceiling decoration (after designs by

*The vault of the atrium,* a splendid gallery glowing with mosaics; below: *the "Genesis" dome with scenes of the Creation of the World.*

Pordenone) in 1549. The mosaics represent the *Resurrection of Lazarus,* the *Crucifixion,* the *Deposition,* and the *Death of the Virgin,* with *Evangelists* and *Prophets* in the spandrels.

The red marble slab on the pavement marks the exact spot where the Emperor Frederick Barbarossa fell to his knees before Pope Alexander III on July 23, 1177.

**14** - Fifteen marvelous Scenes from the *Life of Noah* and the *Flood* decorate the inside of the archway. On the outside is the niche *tomb of Doge Vitale Falier* who died in 1096.

**15** - The bronze panels of the **Porta San Clemente** are divided into 28 rectangular sections, each bearing a figure of a saint beneath which is a Greek inscrip-

tion in silver (a Byzantine work executed in Constantinople). In the lunette is another mosaic by Valerio Zuccato of *St. Clement,* dated 1532. The three-part dome

is decorated with mosaics dated c. 1230. They represent various episodes of *Genesis*, from the *Creation of Heaven and Earth* and the *Creation of Adam and Eve*, up to the *Story of Cain and Abel*.

**16** - The main entrance to the church. On the left is a door leading to the upper galleries and the museum.

## INTERIOR OF THE CHURCH

What makes the interior of the church so striking is the unusual combination of simple architectural forms and an incomparable wealth of decorative motifs. The plan of the building, a Greek cross, has single aisles set off by round arches upon marble

*An allover view of the interior of the Basilica.*

columns, mostly Byzantine in style, and gilded capitals. Five huge domes sustained by massive pillars crown the whole. The patterned flooring made of colored marble dates from the 12th century. Its unevenness is due to the shifting of the structure which rests on pylons. The church including the vestibule, is c. 249 feet long and c. 203 feet at the crossing; the center dome is c. 139 feet on the outside, and c. 91 on the inside.

The Doge supposedly told the unknown architect about to start work on the project that it should be the most beautiful building ever built. And so it was a vision of 4000 m2 of glittery gilding and mosaics upon gold ground. The mosaic work was carried out by Venetian craftsmen in various campaigns. Noteworthy was the contribution of great Renaissance masters from Tuscany. The whole decorative scheme pivots around the theme of the glorification of the Church of the Savior. It would be practically impossible to describe all the mosaics, sculptures, and architectural elements in St. Mark's, so we shall proceed only with a description of the highlights. However, we recommend going to the upper galleries to best view the mosaics.

**17** - Above the center portal is a 14th century mosaic of *Christ Blessing Between the Virgin and St Mark*. In the arch above is a grandiose mosaic of the *Apocalypse According to St. John* by Pordenone and Zuccato (1570-1589). Behind the Apocalypse, against the center window, is the **Arcone del Paradiso** (Arch of Paradise) with Scenes of the *Last Judgement* executed in the 16th and 17th

*Paradise and the Triumph of the Trinity,* mosaic by G. Pilotti.
Opposite page: *the "Capital of the Crucifix",* a hexagonal edicula with two 14th century statues portraying the *Annunciation.*

centuries. Major artists such as Jacopo Tintoretto, Antonio Vassillacchi, Maffeo da Verona, and Domenico Tintoretto contributed to the huge undertaking.

### 18 - THE PENTECOST DOME

In the center is the white dove symbolizing the Holy Spirit whose divine breath spreads out in the form of tongues of fire over the seated Apostles. Between the tiny arched windows are representations of the *Nations of Christendom* and, in the spandrels, monumental *Angels*. These mosaics date from the first half of the 12th century.

### 19 - LEFT AISLE

The mosaics depict *Christ and Four Prophets* (13th century). Among the precious marbles adorning the wall are *Paradise and the Triumph of the Trinity* by G. Pilotti and the *Martyrdom of Apostles Peter and Paul* by Palma the Younger and Padovanino. The right arch contains the *Crucifixion of St. Andrew* by Aliense and the *Murder of St. Thomas* by Tizianello, the left one the *Miracles of St. John* by Patavino. These mosaics all date from the 17th century.

### 20 - THE CAPITAL OF THE CRUCIFIX

This is a hexagonal shrine of six precious marble columns surmounted by carved Byzantine capitals. Inside is a panel painting showing a *Crucifixion* which probably came from Constantinople. According to a legend, it supposedly bled when a maniac attacked it with a knife.

### 21 - THE GREAT WESTERN ARCH

The 12th century mosaic decoration has a dramatic rendition of *Scenes of the Passion*. The episodes are shown in five separate compartments. The dramatic *Crucifixion* scenes are especially noteworthy.

### 22 - On the ceiling and wall are fine mosaics with Scenes of the *Life of the Virgin* and the *Childhood of Christ*. The ceiling mosaics date from the 13th-14th centuries, those on the wall are 16th century works. Jacopo Tintoretto and Palma the Younger took part in the project.

*The Chapel of St. Isidore.*

## 23 - THE CHAPEL OF THE MASCOLI

Founded in 1430, it got its name in 1618 when it belonged to an all male religious confraternity. The sculptures have been ascribed to the Bon family. The fine mosaics, executed between 1430 and 1450, show Scenes from the *Life of the Virgin*.

The two lefthand episodes are by Michele Giambono and the *Visitation* and the *Death of the Virgin* on the right were executed after cartoons by Jacopo Bellini and Andrea Mantegna.

*The Madonna Nicopeia*, the most venerated image in St. Mark's Basilica.

## 24 - THE CHAPEL OF ST. ISIDORE

The chapel was commissioned by Doge Andrea Dandolo between 1354 and 1355 to contain the mortal *remains of St. Isidore* which have been placed on the altar in a Venetian-Gothic sculpted urn. The 14th century mosaics covering the walls and ceiling show fifteen episodes from the *Life of St. Isidore* rendered in a lively narrative style.

## 25 - THE DOME OF ST. JOHN

It is adorned with 13th century mosaics in the Venetian-Gothic style showing Romanesque influence. The mosaics portray Scenes from the *Life of John* with four saints in the spandrels. Two of the saints, *Gregory and Jerome*, are by Giambattista Piazzetta.

## 26 - THE CHAPEL OF THE MADONNA NICOPEIA

Before entering the chapel, do not overlook the *Altar of St. Paul*, an exquisite Renaissance sculpture against the lefthand pillar. The carved altar frontal showing the *Conversion of St. Paul* has been attributed to Pietro Lombardo. The *statue of St. Paul* on the altar is in the style of Lombardo. The chapel con-

*View of the old crypt of the basilica, dating to the 11th century.*
Opposite page, above: ***another view of the crypt; below: St. Peter,*** a mosaic in the vault of the apse in the chapel of St. Peter (13th century).

tains the image of the *Madonna Nicopeia* (the Virgin Victorious) which is greatly venerated by the Venetians who consider her their protectress. The image, actually a Byzantine painting with Oriental enameling predating the year 1000, was brought to Venice from Constantinople by Doge Enrico Dandolo in 1204. The altar is by Tommaso Contino (1617), while the sculptures of the *Virgin and Saints* are 11th and 12th century Venetian-Gothic. The decorative mosaics beneath the arches were done over in the 17th century.

## 27 - THE GREAT NORTH ARCH

The mosaics represent the *Wedding at Cana* and *Supper in the House of Simon* (after cartoons by Jacopo Tintoretto), *Christ Healing the Leper* by P.Veronese, and the *Healing of the Sick Man* and the *Resurrection of the Son of the Widow Naim* by Giuseppe Salviati. In the small arch are four *prophets*.

## 28 - THE CRYPT OF ST. MARK

The crypt beneath the choir, reached by a flight of stairs, has ribbed vaults upon Greek and Byzantine columns. The mortal remains of St. Mark were laid to rest here in 1094, but were later removed since the crypt, lying below the lagoon water level, was

*The Chapel of St. Peter; on the altar, St. Peter worshipped by two "procurators",*
*bas-relief, 14th century.*

subject to periodic flooding. After extensive alteration, it was completely dried out and reopened to worship in 1889.

## 29 - THE CHAPEL OF ST. PETER

Before the actual chapel is an "iconostasis" (rood screen) with five sculpted saints attributed to the school of the Dalle Masegne family. The relief of St. Peter on the smaller altar is a 14th century Venetian school work. The mosaics covering the walls portray *Scenes from the Lives of St. Mark and St. Peter* (2nd half of the 13th century). A door behind the altar of St. Peter leads to the **Sacristy**, while the one on the lefthand side leads to the church of San Teodoro. The lovely Sacristy with its mosaic ceiling was built in 1486. The *Christ* in the center of the ceiling is probably by Titian, the *four Evangelists* around him and several figures of *Apostles* in the lunette of the righthand wall have been attributed to Lorenzo Lotto, and, in the recess of the portal, the figure of *God the Father* is by Padovanino. On either side of the portal are two figures of *St. Jerome*, pieces submitted to a competition held in 1563, by Domenico Bianchini known as "Il Rosso" (the Redhead) and his nephew, Giannantonio. The inlays on the three finely-executed cabinets portray Scenes from the *Life of St. Mark*, *Still-lifes*, and *Landscapes*. Although crafted by several different artists, they seem to have an overall compositional pattern inspired by a single master whose style recalls Vittore Carpaccio's. In fact art historians believe that the extraordinary panels were based on Carpaccio cartoons. The **Chiesetta di San Teodoro**, now part of the sacristy, is in Renaissance style. In the past it was the headquarters of the Inquisition Court. Over the altar are sculptures by Sansovino and, on the wall, a mosaic of *St. John the Beggar* by Pietro Vecchia. To the left of the altar is the entrance to the **Aula Capitolare** (Chapter Room) containing a number of noteworthy paintings such as the *Adoration of the Shepherds* by G. B. Tiepolo and *Portraits of confraternity directors* by followers of Gentile Bellini, Titian, B. Strozzi and Pietro Longhi.

## 30 - THE APSE

The apse is entered through the **Chapel of St. Peter**. The Byzantine mosaics between the windows, untouched by the fire of 1106, are the oldest in St. Mark's. They represent *Sts. Nicholas, Peter, Mark*, and *Hermagora*. The door leading to the sacristy is by Sansovino.

## 31 - THE MAIN ALTAR AND CHOIR DOME

The main altar is surmounted by a tribune resting upon four precious columns made of Oriental albaster and covered with reliefs depicting Scenes from the *Lives of Christ and Mary* sculpted by 13th century Venetian masters. Above are statues of the *Savior* and the *four Evangelists*. To the left of the Ciborium are four bronze sculptures representing the *Evangelists* by Sansovino and the four statues opposite them are

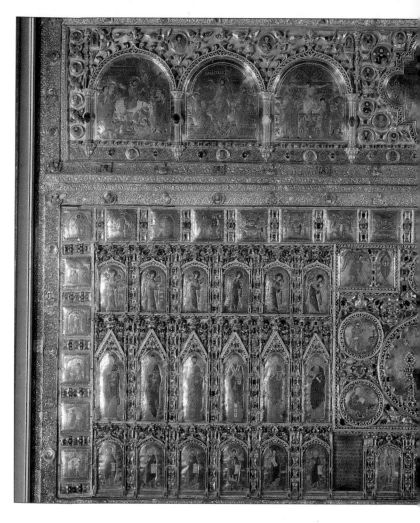

*The Pala d'Oro, the golden altarpiece.*

the *Fathers of the Church* sculpted by Girolamo Paliari in 1614. Inside the main altar are the relics of the Evangelist Mark, while over it is the celebrated masterpiece of Medieval goldsmithing the **Pala d'Oro**, by the Venetian master Giampaolo Boninsegna (1345). 10 feet long and almost 5 feet tall, it was originally commissioned from artists in Constantinople in 978, then embellished in 1105 with gold and enamels brought to Venice after the Fourth Crusade, of 1204 from the Monastery of the Pantocrator. Boninsegna is also responsible for the embossing and setting the gemstones. The Pala has eighty enamel plaques which illustrate Scenes from the *Lives of Christ*, the *Virgin*, and *St. Mark*, as well as figures of *angels*, *prophets*, the *Evangelists*, and *Oriental empe-*

*rors.* The choir dome is covered with a mosaic of *Christ Pantocrator,* the *Virgin and Prophets,* with the figures of the *Evangelists* in the spandrels.

### 32 - THE GREAT EASTERN ARCH

Opposite the main altar is an impressive rood screen. This consists of a colored marble railing on top of which eight columns support an architrave with statues of *St. Mark,* the *Virgin,* and the *Apostles.* The fourteen statues are by Jacobello and Pier Paolo Dalle Masegne (1394). The bronze and silver *Crucifix* in the center is by Jacopo and Marco Bennato. On either side of the choir are elaborate inlaid stalls crafted by a Jesuit, Fra Vincenzo, and four lecterns decorated with bronzes by Sansovino. In the overhead arch

*The main altar of the Basilica.* Opposite page: *Christ Enthroned, Giving His Blessing,* detail of the mosaic in the semi-dome in the apse over the main altar.

are mosaics with New Testament Scenes from the *Life of Christ* executed after cartoons by Jacopo Tintoretto. The Doge and magistrates attended services here in the choir.

**33** - On either side of the rood screen are two ambos (pulpits). On the left is the so-called **double ambo** dating from the 14th century: the lower one, for readings from the Epistles, is an eight- sided structure resting on eleven columns made of precious marble, while the upper one, for readings from the Gospel, rests upon seven columns and is covered with a gilded bronze dome. The ambo on the right is known as the **Pulpito della Reliquia** since on major feast-days relics of the saints were shown from it. Here the newly-elected Doge was presented to the people. The statue of the *Virgin* above has been attributed to Giovanni Bon.

## **34** -THE DOME OF THE ASCENSION

It is decorated with a 13th century Byzantine mosaic in which western influence can be felt. The mosaic shows *Christ in Glory* surrounded by fluttering *angels* with the *Virgin* and *Apostles* assembled below. Between the windows are personifications of the sixteen *Virtues* that were essential characteristics of the living Christ. Figures of the *Evangelists* and the *four sacred rivers* mentioned in the Bible adorn the spandrels.

## **35** - THE GREAT SOUTHERN ARCH

The subjects of these superb 13th century mosaics are *Jesus Entering Jerusalem*, the *Temptation of Christ*, the *Last Supper*, and the *Washing of the Feet*. The *God the Father in Glory* in the center is a 17th century work by Giacomo Pasterini.

## **36** - THE CHAPEL OF ST. CLEMENT

This chapel, like the choir, is preceded by a red marble rood screen. Four columns support an architrave adorned with statues sculpted by the Dalle Masegnes in 1397. The relief on the altar depicting the *Virgin* is by Pirgotele (1465). The Doge could hear Mass without being seen by listening at the barred window to the right of the altar. On the left is a *reliquary* also sculpted by the Dalle Masegnes. The scenes illustrated in the ceiling are the *Removal of the Body of St. Mark from Alexandria*, the *Departure from Egypt*, and the *Arrival in Venice*. The mosaics beyond the organ with Scenes from the *Life of St. Clement* date from the 13th century.

## 37 - THE ALTAR OF THE BLESSED SACRAMENT

In front of the altar is a pair of bronze *candlesticks* by Maffeo Olivieri (1527). On the right is a 15th century relief depicting *St. Peter amidst the worshippers* and, on the left, a Byzantine *Virgin*. Against a column is an *Angel* in front of which burns an eternal light in memory of the prodigious discovery of the body of St. Mark. The mosaics in the arch depict the *Parables and Miracles of Christ*, whereas those covering the wall above the altar and between the windows illustrate *Scenes from the Life of St. Leonard* to whom the altar had originally been dedicated. Pietro Vecchia is the author of the mosaics.

## 38 - THE DOME OF ST. LEONARD

These 13th century mosaics contain images of several saints greatly venerated by the Venetians: *Sts. Leonard, Nicholas, Biagio* and *Tecla* by Vincenzo Bastiani (1512). Under the small inner arch are other 15th mosaics with figures of *saints*. On the outer one around the Gothic rose-window dating from the 15th century are fine mosaics narrating the *Miracles of Christ* by G. Pauletti. The Doge entered the church through the door beneath the rose-window.

## 39 - THE RIGHT TRANSEPT

At the far side is the entrance to the Treasury. Over the door is a 13th century Moorish arch. In a lunette between two mosaic *angels* is a 14th century *Ecce Homo*. Underneath the lefthand arches are mosaic renderings of *Sts. Geminiano* and *Saverio*.

## 40 - THE TREASURY OF ST. MARK

Preceding the treasury is the so-called "Sanctuary" which has a collection of 110 reliquaries as well as other sacred pieces.

The Treasury contains the relics and precious artifacts that the Venetians acquired through trade or as war booty over the centuries.

Preceding page: *the Chapel of St. Clement.*
Left: *some of the precious objects in the Treasury of St. Mark's Basilica.*

*View of the vaults and lunettes of the Baptistry with 14th century mosaics;* in the foreground, *the statue of St. John the Baptist,* by Francesco Segala.

## 41 - THE RIGHT HAND AISLE

The right wall is covered with superb Venetian school mosaics showing both Byzantine and Romanesque influence. They represent the *Virgin in Prayer and Four Prophets* (1230). Beneath the last arch is a huge *holy water font* composed of a basin carved out of a single piece of porphyry and decorated with sculptures by the Lombardos.

## 42 - BATTISTERO

The Venetians call it "Chiesa dei Putti" (Church of the Putti), since infants are baptized here. Doge Andrea Dandolo (who is buried here) commissioned it in 1350. The huge *baptismal font* was designed by Jacopo Sansovino and beautifully crafted by Desiderio Fiorentino, Tiziano Minio, and Francesco Segala. The bronze lid is decorated with figures of *Evangelists* and Scenes from the *Life of St. John the Baptist*. The statuette of St. John the Baptist is also by Segala (1575). Before the altar is the tomb of one of the Venetian greats, Jacopo Sansovino, a gilded silver altar front embossed with figures of *Saints* and 13th and 14th century Byzantine reliefs protraying the *Baptism of Christ* and *Sts. George and Theodore*. Here too the ceilings, lunettes, and domes are adorned with 14th century mosaics. The finest of these are *Christ and the Apostles Preaching the Gospel* and the *Herod's Banquet* (on the dome), *Christ in Glory Amidst the Heavenly Hosts* (on the dome above the altar) and Scenes from the Life of *St. John the Baptist* and the *Crucifixion* (on the lunettes and walls).

## 43 - THE ZEN CHAPEL

The Republic decreed the erection of this superb chapel in memory of Cardinal G. Battista Zen who, before he died in 1501, bequeathed a rich legacy to his native city. The *Cardinal's tomb* in the center was cast in bronze by Paolo Savin. The other sculptures and bronzes are by Savin and others (Pietro Campanato, A. Leonardi, and A. Lombardo). On the bronze altar is a statue, also in bronze, known as the "*Virgin of the Shoe*", since, according to a legend, a shoe donated to the image by a poor man miraculously turned into solid gold. The 14th century mosaics recount the *Life of St Mark*. In the apse semidome is the *Virgin and Child with Angels* while on the wall is a Byzantine relief, with a Greek inscription, of another *Virgin*. In Lombard-style niches are lovely statuettes of four *prophets*, a superb Venetian-Romanesque *Nativity* and, on either side of the altar, a pair of marble *lions*.

Retracing our steps, we return to the atrium where we climb the stairs to the **MARCIANO MUSEUM** which has a superb collection of tapestries, rugs, old lace, and other works of art. The highlights are: the organ panels by Gentile Bellini, ten tapestries with Scenes from the *Passion of Christ* (after designs by Zannino di Pietro), four tapestries with Stories from the *Life of St. Mark* (executed in 1551 after designs by Sansovino) and an *altarpiece* by Paolo Veneziano dated 1345. One of Veneziano's masterpieces, the altarpiece once served as the cover for the Pala d'Oro in the main altar and has Scenes from the *Life of St Mark*, the *Dead Christ* and the *Virgin and Saints*.

The name of the architect who designed this remarkable building has been lost, but whoever it was made it the symbol of the supreme power and glory of the Republic of St. Mark. On this site, towards the end of the 9th century, Doges Angelo and Giustiniano Partecipazio established the seat of the government which came to be known as the "Palazzo Ducale" (Doges' Palace), since it was the residence of the Doge, the supreme head of state. However, the impressive structure we see today retains nothing of its 9th century origins. In fact, before the year 1000, when it was a Byzantine palace built over pre-existing Roman walls, the 9th century building was gutted in a fire. It was rebuilt a number of times, until 1340, when it assumed its present-day form. Actually, tradition ascribes the building of the 14th century palace to Filippo Calandario, stone-cutter, Pietro Baseio, and Master Enrico. The façade overlooking the lagoon was completed between 1400-1404, whereas the Piazzetta side was not ready until 1424. Although renowned Florentine and Lombard masters were called in to decorate the prestigious building, most of the ornamental design in the elaborate Flamboyant Gothic style was handled by a Venetian family of artists who were highly skilled marble craftsmen, the Bons. The result is this incredible building, seemingly suspended over the double tier of arcading which gives it such an airy effect. Then in 1577 another fire broke out, burning down an entire wing. Another competition for its reconstruction was announced and entries from the most celebrated architects of the day poured in. The project by Antonio Da Ponte, architect of the Rialto Bridge, was selected and the building was restored to its 14th century appearance.

*The Judgement of Solomon*, attributed to Pietro Lamberti or Nanni di Bartolo.

*The Doges' Palace;* below: *the balcony on the western façade of the Doges' Palace,* school of Sansovino, with the *statue of Venice in the Robes of Justice,* by A. Vittoria and the *statue of the Doge Andrea Gritti before the Symbol of Venice,* by U. Botasso.

## THE FAÇADES

A person approaching the palace from the canal perceives it like a fairytale mirage, with its delicate pink and white patterned walls and its seemingly weightless architectural structure. The façade is symmetrically broken up by the lovely carved balcony built by Pier Paolo and Jacobello Dalle Masegne in true Flamboyant Gothic style (that is, with elaborate sculptural decoration). Rising above the whole is a *statue of Venice* in the *Robes of Justice,* a 16th century work by Alessandro Vittoria. Worthy of attention amongst the elegant carved capitals of the arcade columns is the first one on the Piazzetta side representing *Adam and Eve in the Garden of Eden* (early 15th century). The west façade facing the Piazzetta closely resembles the south (canal) side, with a balcony erected by pupils of Sansovino in 1536 imitating the one designed by the Dalle Massegnes. Over the pointed arch window is a panel with *Doge Andrea Gritti before the symbol of Venice*, a modern work by Ugo Botasso, and, on the very top, a statue of *Justice* by Alessandro Vittoria.

Right by the façade of the church of St. Mark on the Piazzetta side is the so-called **Porta della Carta**, literally the Charter Portal, to which government decrees were affixed. It originally was known as the "golden portal," since it was once decorated in blue and gold. The upper section, elaborately carved as befits the Flamboyant Gothic taste, is the work of the Bon family. Just above the doorway is a statue of *Doge Foscari Kneeling before the Winged Lion* (modern), while the woman seated above the tallest spire represents *Justice*. On the corner of the Doges' Palace is a famous sculptural group depicting the *Judgement of Solomon*. This extraordinary 15th century sculpture has been attributed to either Pietro Lamberti or Nanni di Bartolo.

## THE INTERIOR

Now that the damage caused by the popular uprising of 1797 at the time of the French occupation has been repaired, the interior of the Doges' Palace and all of the art masterpieces it contains have been restored to their former splendor. Here for hundreds of years the Doges and high-ranking officials of the Republic vied in accumulating extraordinary pieces to adorn these rooms in which the most important deci-

Preceding page: *the courtyard of the Doges' Palace.* Above: *the Renaissance wing of the courtyard;* below, top to bottom: *two bronze well curbs,* by Niccolò dei Conti and by Alfonso Alberghetti.

sions regarding the life of the city were made. Today, all kinds of cultural events are held inside the palace itself or in the courtyard, which makes a unique setting for the nighttime concerts held throughout summer.

## THE COURTYARD

The Porta della Carta brings us to the **Foscari Portico** which we cross to enter the courtyard of the Doges' Palace. Its effect is both peaceful and majestic. In the middle is a pair of imposing bronze *well-curbs.* The one closer to the

*The Staircase of the Giants.*
Opposite page: *the statues of Mars and Neptune,* by Sansovino.

portal is by Alfonso Alberghetti (1559), while the other is by Niccolò dei Conti (1556), both of whom worked as cannon forgers for the Republic of St. Mark. The main or eastern façade (facing the entrance) was designed by Antonio Rizzo at the end of the 15th century. Its pleasing esthetic effect is largely a result of the harmony of the architectural elements achieved by combining the lower, Gothic, section with the upper, Renaissance, level. If you think about it such bold blending of different styles is a hallmark of

Venetian architecture and one of the reasons for its special charm. The elaborate decorative scheme is by Pietro Lombardo (15th century).

The right side was designed by Scarpagnino in the mid 1500s, whereas the two brick façades which border the courtyard on the south and west sides were built by Bartolomeo Manopola in the 17th century as imitations of the outer façades.

The arches of the north façade, on top of which is a giant clock, are broken up by niches with restored Antique statues inside them, another Baroque creation by Manopola. To the right, set on a tall base, is a *monument to Francesco Maria I della Rovere*,

Duke of Urbino sculpted by Giovanni Bandini in 1587. By the Staircase of the Giants is the **Foscari Arch**, begun by the Bons in the Gothic style, and later finished by Rizzo and the Bregnos according to the Renaissance taste. Along the top of the structure are statues of *St. Mark* and other allegorical figures. The niches below contain statues of *Adam and Eve*, bronze copies of Antonio Rizzo's originals now inside the palace. Alongside the Staircase of the Giants is the tiny **Courtyard of the Senators** where the senators of the Republic supposedly assembled during official ceremonies. The **Staircase of the Giants** received its name from the two colossal statues of *Mars* and

*Neptune* on either side of the landing. The statues are by Sansovino and his pupils; the overall project, however, was designed by Antonio Rizzo at the end of the 15th century. The new doges were officially crowned on the landing at the top of the stairs. Having climbed the staircase we are on the second floor loggia.

## THE FIRST FLOOR (OR PIANO NOBILE)

To reach the upper floors of the palace we take the **Scala d'Oro**, literally, the Golden Staircase, designed by Sansovino in 1538 for Doge Andrea Gritti, but completed by Scarpagnino in 1559. The staircase, with a barrel vault ceiling covered with splendid gilded stucco reliefs was originally reserved for the VIPs of the day. The first arch at the entrance is decorated with two sculptures by Tiziano Aspetti (2nd half of the 16th century) portraying *Hercules* and *Atlas*. Two statues

by Francesco Segala symbolizing *Abundance* and *Charity* decorate the third floor. The second floor, which served as the doges' private apartments, was first occupied by Doge Agostino Barbarigo towards the end of the 15th century, as it had to be completely rebuilt after the 1483 fire (the architects commissioned were Antonio Rizzo and Pietro Lombardo).

### THE SALA DEGLI SCARLATTI (THE SCARLATTI ROOM)

The room received its name since all of the high-ranking members of the doge's entourage wore scarlet on official occasions. The splendid ceiling decoration of a gold pattern against a blue ground was executed by Biagio and Pietro da Faenza in 1505. The Lombardos sculpted the fireplace on which you can see the coat-of-arms of the Barbarigo family. The stucco relief depicting the *Virgin and Child* is a Paduan school work. Opposite is a relief representing *Doge Leonardo*

*The Scarlatti Room.*

1 - The Scala d'Oro (Golden Staircase)
2 - Scarlatti Room
3 - Shield Room
4 - Grimani Room
5 - Erizzo Room
6 - Stucco Room
7 - Philosophers' Room
8 - The Doge's private apartments
(Painting Collection)
9 - Room of theQuarantia Criminal
10 - Anteroom of the Maggior
Consiglio
11 - Room of the Quarantia Civil
Vecchia

12 - Guariento Room
13 - Room of the Great Council
14 - Room of the Quarantia Civil
Nuova
15 - Voting Room
16 - Room of the Censors

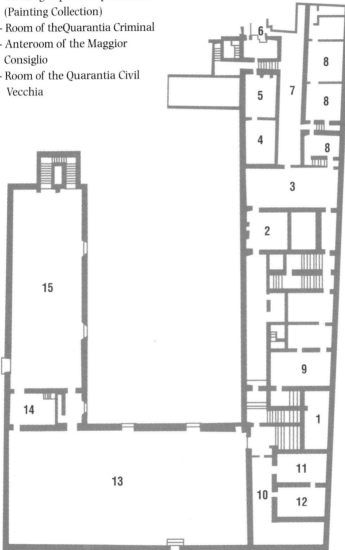

Right: *the Scala d'Oro - Golden Staircase.*
Opposite: *the Lion of St Mark*

*Loredan Presented to the Virgin by St. Mark,* that shows the influence of Pietro Lombardo's style.

## THE SALA DELLO SCUDO
### (THE SHIELD ROOM)

The shield belonging to Venice's last doge was preserved here and thus the room's name. In addition, it once served as an assembly hall for the doge's private guards. The maps around it were made in 1762 by F.

Grisellini who based himself on existing maps made prior to 1540.

## THE SALA GRIMANI
### (THE GRIMANI ROOM)

In the center of the ceiling is the coat-of-arms of the Grimani family after whom the room was named. The painted frieze just below the ceiling which has been attributed to Andrea Vicentino consists of panels with allegorical scenes. The marble

fireplace was sculpted at the beginning of the 16th century by Tullio and Antonio Lombardo.

### THE SALA ERIZZO
### (THE ERIZZO ROOM)

On the fireplace is the coat-of-arms of Doge Erizzo. The carved ceiling dates from the 16th century. From the adjoining terrace, transformed into a hanging garden, there is a fine view over the courtyard.

### THE SALA DEGLI STUCCHI
### (THE STUCCO ROOM)

The stucco decoration dates from the time of the dogeship of Marino Grimani. Several noteworthy paintings are hanging here: an *Adoration of the Magi* by Bonifacio de' Pitati, a *Portrait of Henry III* by Tintoretto, an *Adoration of the Shepherds* by Leandro Bassano, and a *Holy Family* by Salviati.

### THE SALA DEI FILOSOFI
### (THE PHILOSOPHERS' ROOM)

Twelve portraits of philosophers by Veronese and Tintoretto, now in Sansovino's Library, originally hung here. A long corridor leads to the doge's private chapel whose door is adorned with a *St. Christopher*, a fine work by Titian.

### THE PAINTING COLLECTION

These three rooms, once part of the doge's private suite, overlook the little canal behind the Doges' Palace. Noteworthy are the 15th century fireplaces with the Barbarigo coat-of-arms. The paintings, once hung

1 - Square Atrium
2 - Room of the Four Doors
3 - Antechamber
4 - Council Chamber
5 - Senate Chamber
6 - Chapel Antechamber
7 - Chapel
8 - Corridor
9 - Room of the Council of Ten
10 - Compass Room
11 - Room of the Heads of the
    Council of Ten
12 - Inquisitors' Room
13 - Staircase of the Censors
14 - Salles d'Armes of the
    Council of Ten

elsewhere, include a *Lamentation* by Giovanni Bellini in the first room and Carpaccio's famous *Lion of St Mark* of 1516 with an interesting view of the harbor of St. Mark's in the background. In the second are paintings by the famous 16th century Flemish painter, Bosch. The two panel paintings represent *Heaven and Hell,* while the two altarpieces show the *Temptation of Sts. Jerome, Anthony and Egidius* and the *Martyrdom of St. Juliana.* These paintings called "stregozzi" (spell-binders) are typical examples of Bosch's striking fantasy. In the third room is a *Virgin and Child* by Boccaccino and a *Lamentation* by Antoniello da Saliba.

*Mercury and the Three Graces,* by J. Tintoretto.

### THE SALA DEGLI SCUDIERI (THE SQUIRES' ROOM)

This room is reached through the Map Room. The works on display include *Venice Receiving the Homage of Neptune* by Tiepolo, the *Annunciation* by Palma the Younger, and three allegorical paintings by Tintoretto.

## SECOND PIANO NOBILE

*Vulcan's Forge,* by J. Tintoretto.

We retrace our steps to the Scala d'Oro and go up a flight. The third floor occupies the whole east wing of the building and was rebuilt over a long period after being destroyed by fire.

### THE ATRIO QUADRATO (THE SQUARE ATRIUM)

The octagonal painting in the center of the carved wooden ceiling of *Doge Gerolamo Priuli Receiving the Sword and Scales from Justice* by Tintoretto shows the master's skill in

*Bacchus and Ariadne,* by J. Tintoretto

achieving striking compositional and coloristic effects. Two of the several noteworthy paintings displayed here are *Adam and Eve* and the *Prayer in the Garden*, both by Veronese.

## THE SALA DELLE QUATTRO PORTE
### (THE ROOM OF THE FOUR DOORS)

This was once the assembly hall of the Collegio (Council), but it later served as a special anteroom to the Senate Chamber. Built by Antonio Da Ponte after a design by Andrea Palladio, it has elaborate gold and white stucco decoration. The subjects of the paintings are allegorical representations of the power and glory of the Venetian republic. Of special note are the allegorical ceiling frescos by Tintoretto and the celebrated painting of *Doge Antonio Grimani Kneeling before Faith in the Presence of St. Mark* by Titian.

## THE ANTICOLLEGIO
### (THE ANTECHAMBER)

People waiting to be received by the doge assembled here. On the ceiling is *Venice Distributing Honors and Rewards* by Veronese. The elaborate fireplace was designed by Vincenzo Scamozzi. Four masterpieces by Tintoretto adorn the walls: *Vulcan's Forge*, *Mercury and the Three Graces*, *Bacchus and Arianna*, and *Minerva Dismissing Mars*. Veronese painted the much-restored *Rape of Europa*.

## THE SALA DEL COLLEGIO
### (THE COUNCIL CHAMBER)

This is where the doge and the highranking magistrates held audiences and discussed affairs of state. The room was designed by Palladio and built by Da Ponte. On the ceiling is a superb cycle of paintings by

*Council Chamber.*

Veronese whose skillful treatment of light and harmonious compositional patterns create particularly attractive effects. The subjects of these allegorical paintings are the *Allegory of Faith* (center), *Sacrifice* (below), *Venice Enthroned Crowned by Justice and Peace* (above the tribune), *Mars and Neptune* (above the entrance), and a series of allegorical figures. On the tribune wall is the *Glorification of the Victory of Lepanto* by Veronese, while paintings by Jacopo Tintoretto complete the decorative scheme.

## THE SALA DEL SENATO
### (THE SENATE CHAMBER)

Here the doge presided over the senate meetings. The subjects of the paintings are all related to the glorification of Venice and her

*The Senate Chamber.*

rulers. On the ceiling is Tintoretto's *Venice, Queen of the Seas* and, over the doge's throne, two other Tintorettos, the *Dead Christ* and *Doge Loredan Praying to the Virgin to End the Famine and Concede a Victory over the Turks*. Above the door opposite the throne is a painting by Palma the Younger depicting *Doges Lorenzo and Girolamo Priuli Praying the Savior to End the Plague*. The senators' seats were restored in the 18th century.

## THE ANTICHIESETTA (THE CHAPEL ANTECHAMBER)

The ceiling of this stuccoed room has frescoes by Guarana representing *Allegories of Good Government*. On the walls are the cartoons done by Sebastiano Ricci for the façade of St. Mark's, show-ing the *Arrival of the Body of St. Mark in Venice*.

## THE CHIESETTA (THE CHAPEL)

It was built by Vincenzo Scamozzi in 1593. On the altar is a sculpture of the *Virgin and Child with St. John* by Jacopo Sansovino and on the ceiling are frescoes by Guarana.

## THE SALA DEL CONSIGLIO DEI DIECI (THE ROOM OF THE COUNCIL OF TEN)

In this room the much-feared Ten (magistrates) who were entrusted with security of state held their meetings. The subjects of the paintings all pertain to the council's functions. In the center of the ceiling is a copy of a Veronese, *Jupiter Smiting Vices*.

*Room of the Council of Ten.*
Opposite page, top left and right: *the Compass Room; Room of Henry IV.*

The original carried off by the French in 1797, is presently in the Louvre. *The Old Man in Eastern Dress with a Girl* and *Juno Offers the Doges' Hat to Venice* are by Veronese. In the other compartments are allegorical figures by Ponchino and Zelotti.

### THE SALA DELLA BUSSOLA (THE COMPASS ROOM)

The "compass" is actually the double door leading to the adjoining Sala dei Capi del Consiglio dei Dieci. Here people about to be questioned and the condemned were kept waiting. Along one of the walls you can still see the notorious "bocche di leone" (literally, lions' mouths), actually slots into which citizens could drop anonymous denunciations. The fireplace is by

Sansovino and his helpers. On the ceiling is a copy of a Veronese, *St. Mark and the Virtues*, the original of which is in the Louvre.

### THE SALA DEI TRE CAPI DEL CONSIGLIO DEI DIECI (ROOM OF THE THREE HEADS OF THE COUNCIL OF TEN)

Of special note are two paintings by Veronese, the *Punishment of the Forger* and *Sin Vanquished by Victory* and the fireplace by Jacopo Sansovino.

### THE SALETTA DEGLI INQUISITORI (THE INQUISITORS' ROOM)

In this room (which directly communicates with the prisons) people were brought before the

Below: *bust of the Doge Sebastiano Venier*, by A. Vittoria.

Inquisition for questioning. The ceiling paintings are by Tintoretto.

### THE LANDING OF THE CENSORS' STAIRCASE

Retracing our steps through the Compass Room we come out by the staircase leading up to the Weapons Rooms.

### THE SALE D'ARMI DEL CONSIGLIO DEI DIECI (THE SALLES D'ARMES ROOMS OF THE COUNCIL OF TEN)

In the past these rooms

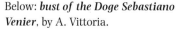

were used as prisons, but starting from the early 14th century, they were turned into armories. Today they contain a fascinating, easy-to-follow collection of weapons of the past. The objects on display comprise swords (one of which is an especially fine example of 14th century Venetian craftsmanship), pikes, halberds, armor (including the armor worn by Henry IV King of France and two suits of armor that once belonged to the Sforza family), and a twenty-barrel arquebus. Among the sculptures are a marble bust of *Sebastiano Venier*, the hero of the Battle of Lepanto, by Alessandro Vittoria, a bronze bust of *Francesco Morosini* by the Genoese artist Filiberto Parodi, and a bronze bust of *Marcantonio Bragadin* by Tiziano Aspetti.

We return, by way of the **Scala dei Censori**, to the second floor (where we have already visited the doge's private apartments).

We shall now tour the remaining rooms.

*Room of the Quarantia Civil Vecchia.*

*Hall of the Maggior Consiglio.*

## THE ANDITO DEL MAGGIOR CONSIGLIO (THE CORRIDOR OF THE GREAT COUNCIL)

This hallway overlooking the harbor is illuminated by beautiful Gothic windows. On the right wall are works by Palma the Younger; on the left, works by Tintoretto.

## THE SALA DELLA QUARANTIA CIVIL VECCHIA (THE ROOM OF THE FORTY)

This room was the seat of the Supreme Court composed of forty members. It is adorned with allegorical and commemorative paintings.

## THE SALA DEL GUARIENTO (THE GUARIENTO ROOM)

Originally it was called the Armament Room as ammunition was stored here, but now it contains what is left of a masterpiece of art, the *Paradise* fresco by the 14th century Paduan artist, Guariento, which was originally painted for the Sala del Maggior Consiglio. Damaged in the fire of 1577, it was replaced by a painting of the same subject commissioned from Jacopo Tintoretto in 1580. We can appreciate its great beauty from this *Coronation of the Virgin*, peopled with figures of *angels*, *saints*, and *prophets*.

## THE SALA DEL MAGGIOR CONSIGLIO (THE HALL OF THE GREAT COUNCIL)

This incredibly huge hall (it measures 177 feet long, 82 feet wide, and 50 feet high) was used for meetings of the Great Council, the Republic's governing body. Five huge Gothic windows looking out on the harbor, two on the Piazzetta, and two on the courtyard afford splendid views over the lagoon and all the famous sights in the vicinity. After the 1577 fire which destroyed the original hall that had been officially inaugurated by Doge Francesco Foscari in 1423, it was soon rebuilt by Antonio Da Ponte and decorated with iconography created by a Florentine scholar, Girolamo de' Bardi and the Venetian historian, F. Sansovino. Upon entering you are immediately struck by the huge painting above the tribune (measuring 72x22 feet). It represents *Paradise* and was painted by Tintoretto between 1588 and 1590. Although numerous restorations have marred a good deal of the original light and shade contrasts, nothing can harm the impressive monumentality of the compositional pattern. *Christ* and the *Virgin* are surrounded by *saints* artfully placed to mark the picture planes. The overwhelming ceiling composed of thirty-five compartments set in grandiose gilded frames was put up by Cristoforo Sorte between 1578 and 1584. Turning our backs to the platform, we shall now examine the highlights of the ceiling paintings, starting from the ones by the harbor wall and then passing to the right side and back to the Door of the Quarantia Civil Nova. **1** - *Antonio Loredan Commands the Attack to Free Scutari from the Siege of Mohammed II*, by Paolo Veronese. **2** - *The Venetian Army and Navy Conquer Polesella*, by Francesco Bassano. **3** - *Vittore Soranzo and His Fleet Victorious at Argenta (1482) against the Troops of Ercole I d'Este*, by Jacopo Tintoretto and his helpers. **4** - *Jacopo Marcello's Conquest of Gallipoli (1494)*, by Tintoretto. **5** - *Giorgio Cornaro and Bartolo Defeating the Imperial Troops of Maximilian I at Cadore*, by Francesco Bassano. **6** - *Andrea Gritti Reconquering Padua*, by Palma the Younger. **7** - In the oval, *Venice Crowned by Victory Welcomes the Vanquished Peoples and Conquered Provinces*, by Palma the Younger. **8** - In the main panel, *Venice Surrounded by Sea Divinities Hands an Olive Branch to Doge Niccolò Da Ponte*, by Tintoretto. **9** - In the oval, *Apotheosis of Venice*, by Veronese. **10** (courtyard side) - *Pietro Mocenigo Leading the Venetians to Victory at Castelmaggiore*, by Francesco Bassano. **11** - *Stefano Contarini Defeating the Visconti Navy at Riva* in 1440, by Tintoretto. **12** - *The Venetians Led by Francesco Barbaro Helping the City of Brescia Break the Siege of Filippo Maria Visconti*, by Tintoretto. **13** - *Carmagnola Leading the Venetians to Victory at Maclodio* in 1426, by Francesco Bassano. **14** -

*Francesco Bembo Leading the Po Fleet to Victory over Visconti's Troops in Cremona*, by Palma the Younger. The portraits of doges just beneath the ceiling are by Domenico Tintoretto and his helpers. There is also an empty space covered by a black cloth with a Latin inscription that reads: "This is the place of Marin Faliero, beheaded for his crimes" (high treason). The subjects of the paintings along the courtyard wall are related to the struggle between Pope Alexander III and Frederick Barbarossa in which Venice was politically involved. The most interesting are the *Ambassadors Petitioning Barbarossa for Peace*, by followers of Tintoretto (fourth panel from the far side of the room), the *Pope Handing the Sword to the Doge* (fifth panel), and *Frederick Barbarossa Prostrate Before the Pope* by Federico (tenth panel).

## THE SALA DELLA QUARANTIA CIVIL NUOVA (THE ROOM OF THE CIVIL COURT FORTY)

This was the seat of the appeals court for citizens residing on the mainland. The fine gilded beam ceiling dates from the

*Room of the Quarantia Civil Nuova.*

*The Venetian Fleet Prepares to Sail Against Barbarossa,* by F. Bassano.

1500s. Above the tribune, partially lined with gilded leather, is a 15th century *Virgin* on a gold ground. The paintings along the walls represent *Venice and Justice*, by A. Foler, *Venice and Neptune*, the *Virtues*, and *Justice Expelling the Vices*, by G. B. Lorenzetti, and *Justice and Time Strip Truth Naked*, by F. Zaniberti.

*The Voting Room.*

## THE SALA DELLO SCRUTINIO (THE VOTING ROOM)

Starting in 1532, this room was where ballots were cast for the election of the Great Council and where commissioners for the election of the doge met. Before the 1577 fire its walls were adorned with paintings by Tintoretto and Pordenone. After being restored by Antonio Da Ponte in 1587, the great hall was redecorated. The theme of the paintings commissioned was once more the glorification of Venice's triumphs on the high seas, drawn up by erudite scholars. Again, not being able to list each and every work, we shall give only the highlights. In the elaborate gilded ceiling attributed to Sorte is the *Conquest of Padua* by Francesco Bassano; on the entrance wall the *Last Judgement* by Palma the Younger; on the courtyard wall the *Conquest of Zara* by Tintoretto and his helpers, and, above the windows, the *Battle of Lepanto*, by Andrea Vicentino. Beneath the ceiling are portraits of doges, a continuation of the series started in the Sala del Maggior Consiglio. The balcony affords a splendid view over the Piazzetta and the Basilica of St. Mark. At the far end of the room is a grandiose *Triumphal Arch*, inspired by Classical Roman models, which was built in honor of Doge Francesco Morosini by Antonio Tirali (attribution).

## THE SALA DELLA QUARANTIA CRIMINAL (THE ROOM OF THE CRIMINAL COURT FORTY)

Reached from the Censors' Staircase, the room contains a *Lion of St. Mark* by Jacobello del Fiore.

## THE SALA DEL MAGISTRATO AL CRIMINAL AND THE SALA DEL MAGISTRATO ALLE LEGGI
### (THE ROOM OF THE CRIMINAL COURT MAGISTRATE AND THE ROOM OF THE LAW MAGISTRATE)

Antonio Rizzo's original marble sculptures of *Adam* and *Eve* (dated 1470), once in the Foscari Arch of the courtyard, have been placed here.

## THE PRISONS

By the Scala d'Oro, on the east side of the Loggias, is a small door which leads to the prisons and the Bridge of Sighs, which communicated with the Avogaria (magistrates' offices) and other courts. The prisoners were led before their judges via the Bridge of Sighs. Prior to the construction of the Palazzo delle Prigioni (Prison Building), this was known as the Old Prison. It was composed of two sections: the *Piombi* (literally, lead) whose cells were located under a lead roof and the *Pozzi* (wells), dank and dark dungeons below the level of the lagoon in which the most dangerous criminals were kept. The eighteen cells making up the pozzi may be visited by descending a flight of stairs.

We shall now visit the suite of rooms known as the **Avogaria** in the east wing of the Doges' Palace on the same floor as the loggias.

## THE SALA DEI CENSORI
### (THE ROOM OF THE CENSORS)

The room served as offices for the two censori whose job it was to watch over the mores of the nobles and denounce cheating in elections. Around the walls are the coats-of-

*Entrance to the New Prisons.*

arms of 266 *censori* (from 1517 to 1629) and portraits of several of them by Tintoretto and Palma.

## THE SALA DEI NOTAI OR SALA DELL'AVOGARIA (THE ROOM OF THE MAGISTRATES)

The walls are hung with portraits of famous *notai* and *avogadori* and several religious scenes by Leandro Bassano and Tintoretto's followers. On one of the walls hangs an odd clock with only six hours shown on its face. The Avogaria was in charge of the so-called Gold and Silver Books, kept in the adjoining Sala dello Scrigno, which listed the noble families of the city.

## THE SALA DELLA MILIZIA DA MAR (THE ROOM OF THE MILITIA OF THE SEA)

This was the headquarters for the captains in charge of recruiting men for the fleet of the Serenissima. The walls are decorated with 18th century frescoes in Tiepolo's style, one of which, the *Adoration of the Magi* has been attributed to Gian Domenico Tiepolo himself. A small adjoining room once served as the office of

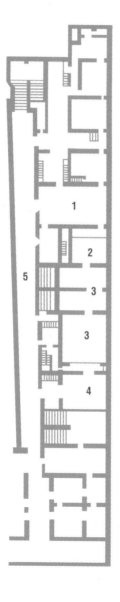

the Segretario alle voci (literally, Secretary of the Items) who was in charge of recording the names of those awarded public office.

### THE SALA DELLA CANCELLERIA DUCALE (THE DOGES' CHANCELLERY)

This room, where the Collegio dei Notai held its meetings, was the office of the Head Chancellor. From here a staircase descends to the pozzi which we have previously described.

The **Museo dell'Opera di Palazzo** (Doges' Palace Museum) - The ground floor museum is well worth a visit. Exhibited here are the original capitals from the palace's outside colonnade, columns, reliefs, pieces of crenellation, and the original architrave from Bartolomeo Bon's Porta della Carta.

Back in the Piazzetta, a glorious view of the harbor can be had from the docks. On the left is the **Ponte della Paglia** where barges transporting straw (paglia) for the prisons docked. Dating to 1360 it was enlarged in the 19th century. On one of the pylons is an image of the gondoleers' protectress, *Our Lady of the Gondoleers*, set inside a 16th century tabernacle.

*Palace of the New Prisons.*

*The Bridge of Sighs.*

## THE BRIDGE OF SIGHS

From the canal side of the Ponte della Paglia you are looking straight at the famous covered bridge, Ponte dei Sospiri, which connects the Doges' Palace and the Prigioni Nuove. Commissioned by Doge Marino Grimano, it was built by Antonio Contini at the turn of the 17th century in the typical Baroque style of the day. The name "Bridge of Sighs" presumably derives from the sighs of the prisoners who had to cross it as they were being brought before the Inquisitors.

## THE RIVA DEGLI SCHIAVONI

A walk down the Riva degli Schiavoni from the Ponte della Paglia along the **Canale di San Marco** (St. Mark's Canal) to the Giardini di Castello (Castle Gardens) is one of the Venetians' favorites. The Riva was once the mooring station for trading vessels coming from Slavonic ports (present-day Dalmatia). Originally no wider than the Ponte della Paglia, it was paved in 1324 and then widened in 1780 by decree of the Senate. Running approximately a third of a mile, today it is a pleasant promenade filled with famous hotels and cafes.

Five hundred years of Venetian art are on exhibit in the Accademia which, for homogenity, clarity of exposition, and quality, cannot be equalled anywhere. Its origins go back to 1750 when the Republic of St. Mark decided to endow the city with an "Accademia di Pittori e scultori" (Academy of Painters and Sculptors) under the direction of Piazzetta. The original Academy occupied the Fondachetto delle Farine (Flour Storehouse), today the Port Authority, situated by the gardens of the former Royal Palace overlooking the harbor of St. Mark. In 1756 the Academy was granted official recognition and Piazzetta, by then an old man, decided to leave it in the capable hands of Giovan Battista Tiepolo. This was the core of the first group of works done by the pupils of the Academy. In 1807, during the French occupation, it was decided to transfer the art school and the works displayed in it to a more fitting place and the choice fell upon the Scuola and Church of the Carità (in the Campo della Carità) and upon the former monastery of the Lateranense Canons, a building designed by Palladio in 1560 (but greatly altered since then). The collection thereafter considerably expanded as numerous works from suppressed churches and monasteries contin-

*Entrance to the Academy (Accademia).*

uously poured in. During the period 1816-1856 bequests from Molin, Contarini, Venier, and Manfrin brought in new treasures. Lastly, several works returned from Austria after the Treaty of St. Germain was signed in 1919, and still other outstanding works were purchased by the Italian State under the directorship of Giulio Cantalamessa and Gino Fogolari. Somebody always asks why the name of the museum is Academy Galleries in the plural, even though there is only a single museum. Actually, the museum originally had two separate sections, one for paintings and the other for plaster casts used by the art students and the plural name has remained.

**ROOM 1** - This splendid room is reached by a monumental staircase built in 1765 and adorned with two fine allegorical statues by Morlaiter. The stupendous gilded carved ceiling frames paintings by Alvise Vivarini and Campagnola. The room is devoted to 14th and 15th century Venetian school paintings. Of special note is the impressive altarpiece by Paolo Veneziano, still full of Byzantine influence. The subjects of the panels are the *Coronation of the Virgin* and Scenes from the *Lives of Christ and St Francis*. Other fine works include the *Coronation of the Virgin* and *Justice between the Archangels Michael and Gabriel* by Jacobello del Fiore (1438) and the *Mystic Marriage of St. Catherine*, plus a superb altarpiece with the *Annunciation, Saints and Prophets* by Lorenzo Veneziano. In the center of the hall is a splendid example of 15th century Venetian goldsmithing, the *Astylar Cross of St. Theodore.*

**ROOM 2** - The late 15th-early 16th century Venetian school. Several of the masterpieces of Giovanni Bellini, renowned for his skillful use of color and feeling for the mystical, are in the Academy collection. These include the *Sacra Conversazione* (originally in the church of San Giobbe) and the *Lamentation.* The *Presentation at the Temple* and *Crucifixion of the 10,000 Martyrs on Mount Ararat* are by Carpaccio.

**ROOM 3** - Cima da Conegliano and Giorgione. The *Female Nude* painted by Giorgione in 1508 is unfortunately in very poor condition.

**ROOM 4** - The major works are

*St. Jerome and a Believer,* by Piero della Francesca (c. 1450).

a *Virgin and Child with Sts. Paul and George,* a *Virgin and Child with Sts. Catherine and Mary Magdalene,*

Above: *St. George,* by A. Mantegna; above, right: *The Virgin of the Zodiac,* by Cosmè Tura (c. 1450); right: *The Tempest,* by Giorgione. Opposite page, top to bottom: *Portrait of a Gentleman,* by L. Lotto; *Pietà,* by G. Bellini.

and a *Virgin with Sleeping Babe* by Giovanni Bellini, the *Virgin of the Zodiac* by Cosme Tura, and *St. Jerome* by Piero della Francesca (c. 1450).

The *St. George* by Mantegna, despite its tiny size, conveys a great sense of monumentality and physical strength.

**ROOM 5** - This room contains Giorgione's splendid much-discussed painting of the *Tempest* full of symbolism and bathed in an atmosphere of lyric melancholy. In addition, there are several more superb Bellinis including the *Madonna degli Alberelli*, the *Pietà*, and the *Virgin and Child with St. John the Baptist and a Female Saint*.

**ROOM 6** - Paris Bordone painted the *Presentation of the Ring to the Doge*, which recounts a mira-cle of St. Mark, against a splendid background showing 16th century Venetian life. Other important works are the *Banquet of the Dives* by Bonifacio de' Pitati, *St. John the Baptist* by Titian, and the *Madonna dei Tesorieri* by Jacopo Tintoretto (1566).

**ROOM 7** - Lorenzo Lotto's *Portrait of a Gentleman* reveals the painter's penetrating insight into the sitter's personality. Savoldo

painted the *St. Anthony the Abbot* with *St. Paul, the Hermit*. The figures convey great solemnity and nobility.

**ROOM 8** - Titian might have had a hand in this *Sacra Conversazione* regarded as Palma the Elder's masterpiece (1525). Also of note are Bonifacio de' Pitati's *Slaughter of the Innocents* and Romanino's *Pietà*.

**ROOM 9** - Titian's school. The most interesting works are *God the Father Blessing Venice* and the *Virgin and Child with Saints* by Bonifacio de' Pitati. The *Evangelists' Symbols* are from Titian's workshop.

**ROOM 10** - The 16th century Venetian school. This room contains several of the museum's major works from the height of the Venetian Renaissance. On of the most striking is the *Banquet in the House of Levi* which Paolo Veronese painted in 1573. The painter had intended this elaborate picture to represent the *Last Supper*, but the Inquisition Court, decreeing that the setting and poses of some of the figures were unbefitting to such a serious subject, compelled him to change the title. The *Miracle of the Slave*, painted by Tintoretto in 1548, was originally part of a whole cycle on the miracle of St. Mark. This work is a splendid example of Tintoretto's skill in using dynamic compositional patterns, emphasized by dramatic treatment of light and shade, which made him one of the greatest of the 16th century Venetian masters. The *Pietà* by Titian, commissioned for the church of the Frari, was the last work the master painted before his death in 1576. The dissolving forms and broader brushstroke are typical of Titian's late style.

**ROOM 11** - The room is divided into two sections. In the first are *Adam and Eve*, the *Creation of the Animals*, and *Cain and Abel* by Tintoretto, and the *Mystic Marriage of St. Catherine* by Veronese. In the second are 16th and 17th century works by painters such as Tiepolo, Luca Giordano, and Pietro da Cortona.

**ROOM 12** - The 17th century Venetian school. The highlights

*Pietà*, by Titian.

*The Rape of Europa*, by F. Zuccarelli.

include several *Landscapes* by Marco Ricci, the *Rape of Europa* by Zuccarelli, and *Landscapes* by Giuseppe Zais.

**ROOM 13** - The most interesting paintings are the *Rest on the Flight to Egypt* and the *Virgin in Glory with St. Jerome* by Jacopo Bassano, the *Virgin and Child and Four Senators* and three *portraits of Procuratori* (magistrates) by Tintoretto, and *Deucalion and Pyrrha, Christ and Pilate*, and the *Presentation in the Temple* by Schiavone.

**ROOM 14** - Noteworthy are several canvases by the Roman painter, Domenico Feti, including *David, Girl Reading, Meditation*, and *Isaac and Jacob*. Jan Liss painted the *Sleeping Turk*, the *Sacrifice of Isaac*, and *Apollo and Marsyas*.

**ROOM 15** - 18th century works by Tiepolo, Solimena, and others.

**ROOM 16** - In addition to superb Tiepolos, this room also contains the *Fortuneteller* by Piazzetta, one of the best-known Venetian genre painters of the 18th century.

**ROOM 17** - Antonio Canale, bet-

*The Fortune Teller,* by G.B. Piazzetta (1740).

ter known as Canaletto, is the foremost painter of the Venetian school called "vedutismo" (views). His pictures, painted in a crystal clear, terse style, appear as mirror-like reflections of reality. Paintings of his favorite subject, views of Venice, can be found throughout European museums. In this room is a *View of Venice* dating from 1765. The other renowned "vedutista" is Francesco Guardi, although his style stressing broad brushstroke and a warm palette differs greatly from Canaletto's. Guardi is represented here by the *View of the Island of San Giorgio*. The delightful genre scenes of everyday life in 18th century Venice are by Pietro Longhi (the *Dancing Lesson*, the *Concert*, the *Toilette*) and Rosalba Carriera (*Self-portrait*, the *French Lady*, and *Portrait of a Youth*). The room also contains a series of attractive drawings by Sebastiano Ricci, Piazzetta, and Giambattista Pittoni.

*St. Jerome,* by J. Bassano (detail).

applied for admission to the Accademia Art School, and a *St. Joseph with Child and Saints* by Tiepolo.

**ROOM 19** - We return to the 15th century. The splendid *Flagellated Christ* is by Antonello da Saliba.

**ROOM 20** - Mostly paintings by Gentile Bellini, Giovanni's brother. Influenced by Mantegna, Gentile loved huge compositions illustrating the magnificence of Venetian public life in the 15th century: the *Processions in Piazza San Marco* (1496) we see here is a fascinating histori-

Above: ***Portico and Courtyard***, by Canaletto;
above: ***View of the Island of S. Giorgio***, by F. Guardi.

**ROOM 18** - 18th century paintings and sculpture. Of special interest are two sculptures, *Apollo* and *Wrestlers*, which are Antonio Canova's trial pieces when, at the age of eighteen, he cal document as well as an outstanding work of art.

The *Miraculous Healing of a Possessed Man* by Vittore Carpaccio reveals the master's extraordinary narrative skill.

*The English Ambassadors at the Court of Brittany,* by V. Carpaccio (c. 1495).

**ROOM 21** - These wall-size paintings are part of a cycle on the theme of the *Legend of St. Ursula* painted by Carpaccio at the end of 1400s (1490-1496) for the Scuola di Sant'Orsola which was suppressed at the time of the French occupation in the late 1790s. The story of Ursula, the virgin princess from Brittany martyred during the Huns' siege of Cologne, is narrated in Carpaccio's inimitable style, combining fanciful flights of imagination with careful observation of down-to-earth everyday detail.

**ROOM 22** - We cross this early 19th century neo-Classical room on our way back to Room 18 from which we enter the huge hall which was once the upper part of the former church of Santa Maria della Carità.

**ROOM 23** - This room features more 15th century paintings. The highlights include Giovanni Bellini's *four triptychs*. Carlo Crivelli's *four saints*, and an altarpiece by Bartolomeo Vivarini depicting the *Nativity, Pietà* and *Angels and Saints*.

**ROOM 24** - Originally the pilgrims' lodgings of the Scuola della Carità, this room has an impressive gilded carved ceiling. The outstanding work on display is undoubtedly Titian's *Presentation in the Temple*. This work was painted in 1538 when Titian had reached full artistic maturity.

# THE MUSEUM OF 18TH CENTURY VENICE

The museum is inside the Palazzo Rezzonico overlooking the Grand Canal. The palace, originally belonging to a noble Venetian family, Rezzonico was the last home of Robert Browning. The City of Venice purchased it in 1935 and used it for the reconstruction of the interior of an 18th century patrician dwelling.

A visit to the museum is the best way to get an idea of what Venice was actually like in the fascinating 1700s, the period so wittily recounted in Carlo Goldoni's plays and on Pietro Longhi's charming canvases.

From the atrium we take the monumental staircase up to the second floor. The first room we see is the huge **Ballroom** adorned with magnificent furniture carved by Brustolon. We then enter the **Sala dell'Allegoria Nuziale** (Room of the Nuptial Allegory) which was named after Tiepolo's painting of the *Marriage of Ludovico Rezzonico*. **The Sala dei Pastelli** (Pastel Room) contains several of Rosalba Carriera's delicate works. In the **Sala degli Arazzi** (Tapestry Room) are splendid Flemish tapestries. The **Sala del Trono** (Throne Room), originally the nuptial chamber, has a fresco in the middle by Tiepolo and, due to the splendor and magnificence of its furnishings, is one of the most elaborate in the palace. The **Sala del Tiepolo** (Tiepolo Room) is adorned with an allegorical fresco by the master representing *Fortune and Wisdom*. The **library** has ceiling paintings by Francesco Maffei. The **Sala del Lazzarini** received its name from

Preceding page: *Palazzo Rezzonico*, home of the Museo del Settecento Veneziano.
Left: *Lacquered "chinoiserie" chest of drawers.*

the two impressive paintings by the Lazzarini adorning it. **The Sala del Brustolon** features the Venetian master-craftsman's exquisite carved furniture and a sculpture collection. Third floor: The **Portego dei Dipinti** (Picture Hall) contains a collection of 18th century Venetian school paintings, including Piazzetta's *Self-portrait* and *Death of Darius*. Jan Liss' *Judith and Holofernes*, and several *Landscapes* by Giuseppe Zais. The **Sala del Longhi** (Longhi Room) contains 34 fascinating genre scenes of 18th century Venetian life by Pietro Longhi. The ceiling painting of *Zephyr and Flora* is by Tiepolo. After passing through two rooms frescoed by Guardi, we enter a delightful reconstruction of an 18th century Venetian bedroom. Two little rooms lead to another reconstruction, this one a re-creation of the Villa dei Tiepolo (Tiepolo Mansion) in Zianigo. These frescoes, all of which originally adorned the villa, are by Domenico Tiepolo, son of Giovan Battista. Also of interest are the **Camera dei Pagliacci** (Clown Room), the **chapel** (frescoed by the young Tiepolo in 1749), and the not-to-be-missed **Sala del Ridotto** which contains two renowned paintings by Guardi, the *Convent Parlor*, and the *Sala del Ridotto*. On the fourth floor is a reconstruction of an old Venetian pharmacy and a **marionette theater**.

# THE FRANCHETTI GALLERY

The palace, along with its furnishings and an extensive collection of paintings of various periods and schools, was donated to the Italian state by Baron Giorgio Franchetti in 1916 and opened to the public in 1927.

Nevertheless, none of the works or rooms bear identification plates or labels in accordance with Baron Franchetti's wish that it retain the appearance of a collection in a private home rather than take on the anonymous look of a state museum.

We shall list only the most significant of the many important works in the collection. In order to make it easier for you to see the gallery, we have numbers for the rooms which, as was previously mentioned, have deliberately been kept "unidentified". In the center of the splendid arcaded courtyard adorned with Roman and Greek sculpture is a fine 15th century marble *well-curb*. By the brick wall, a staircase resting on pointed arches leads up to the second floor loggia, or gallery, along which tapestries and sculpture are displayed. In the **first room** are two works by Carpaccio, the *Annunciation* and the *Death of the Virgin*, originally from the Scuola degli Albanesi, and an altarpiece with the *Passion of Christ* by Antonio Vivarini. In the **second room** is a *Sleeping Venus* by Paris Bordone. In the **third**, a *bust of Benedetto Manzini* by Vittoria. The **fourth room** contains one of the museum's finest works, *Venus at Her Mirror* by Titian. Another masterpiece hangs in the **sixth room**, *St. Sebastian* by Mantegna.

In the **seventh room** on the third floor is a handsome *Portrait of a Gentleman* by Van Dyck. In the **ninth room** the two out-

*View of the Wharf and Punta della Dogana,* by Francesco Guardi.

standing works are Pontormo's *Portrait of a Girl* and Filippo Lippi's *Nativity*. Among the many fine works in the **tenth room** we shall mention two lovely *landscapes* by Francesco Guardi, the *Flagellation* by Luca Signorelli and a noteworthy 15th century *Crucifixion* attributed to Jan Van Eyck. In the **eleventh room** are several Tintoretto portraits and other masterpieces of 16th century painting.

From the third floor we may enter the remaining rooms of the gallery, which are actually part of the adjoining **Palazzo Giusti**; three of them contain Venetian school bronzes and Dutch and Flemish paintings.

## THE QUERINI STAMPALIA MUSEUM

The **Querini Palace**, which also houses the Venice **Public Library**, is located right behind the church of Santa Maria Formosa on Calle Querini.

The picture gallery, featuring Venetian masters from the 14th-18th centuries, occupies twenty rooms on the second floor. The collection also includes rare furniture, china, arms and armor, as well as musical instruments.

**Room 1**, contains curious paintings of *Life in Venice* by Gabriele Bella. **Room 2**, the *Coronation of the Virgin*, by Catarino and Donato Veneziano.

**Room 3**, *portraits*, by Sebastiano Bombelli. **Room 4**, works by Palma the Younger, including *Adam and Eve* and a *Self-portrait*. **Room 5**, Andrea Schiavone, *Conversion of San Paolo* and other three works. **Rooms 6 and 7**, works by Venetian Mannerists, including landscapes, by Matteo de' Pitocchi. **Rooms 8 and 9**, the Renaissance. The highlights here are the *Adoration of the Virgin*, by Lorenzo di Credi, *Sacra Conversazione*, by Palma the Elder, the *Virgin and Child* and *Presentation at the Temple*, by Giovanni Bellini, and *Judith*, by Vincenzo Catena. **Rooms 11-13**, works by Pietro Longhi including the *Seven Sacraments*, *Hunt in the Valley*, and other genre paintings. **Room 14**, Marco Ricci's *landscapes*. **Room 15 through 20**, drawings by Giovanni Bellini, Titian, Raphael, Tintoretto, Veronese, and other masters, in addition to Flemish tapestries, wall hangings, objets d'art, weapons, ceramics, and Louis XVI lacquered furniture. **Room 18**, *Portrait of G. Querini*, by G. Battista Tiepolo. **Room 20**, *Virgin and Child*, by Bernardo Strozzi.

## THE PEGGY GUGGENHEIM COLLECTION

The Peggy Guggenheim Collection is a museum of modern art, established by the American heiress Peggy Guggenheim (1898-1979). She acquired the most important

*Palazzo Venier dei Leoni,* home of the Guggenheim Collection of Modern Art; *below: Untitled,* Kasimir Malevich (c. 1916).

part of the collection (for the purpose of creating a museum of contemporary art) between 1938 and 1947 in London, Paris and New York. In 1942 she opened the gallery-museum Art of This Century in New York, where she exhibited her own collection of European avant-garde works and organized several shows dedicated to young American artists, such as Motherwell, Rothko, Still and Pollock. The collection was shown in Europe for the first time at the Biennale di Venezia in 1948. The following year, Peggy bought the Palazzo Venier dei Leoni, an unfinished XVIII century building on the Grand Canal, where she lived for 30 years, and opened her home to visitors as a museum.

The collection, built up following the advice of artists and critics such as Marcel Duchamp and Herbert Read, and her second husband the German surrealist, Max Ernst, is one of the greatest collections of its kind in the world. In 1976, a few years before she died, Peggy bequeathed the palazzo and the collection to the Solomon R. Guggenheim Foundation, which now manages it along with the Guggenheim museums in New York and Bilbao in Spain.

The Nasher Sculpture Garden contains works by Giacometti (*Woman Standing*), Raymond Duchamp-Villon (*The Horse*) and Henry Moore, Jean Arp and Max Ernst. Two inscriptions behind the gazebo, tell where the ashes of Peggy Guggenheim and her little dogs are buried. In the building, the entrance room contains many important works by Picasso (*On the Beach* and *The Studio*) and a *Mobile* by Alexander Calder. From the entrance we can go to the terrace overlooking the Grand Canal and admire Marino Marini's *The Angel of the City*. Going back inside, the collection continues with important pieces by masters of cubism, Picasso (*The Poet*), Braque (*The Clarinet Player*), Léger, Duchamp, Gris, Gleizes, Metzinger and Delaunay. Early Italian Modernism is represented by the Futurists, (Boccioni, Balla and Severini) and the metaphysical painter Giorgio De Chirico (*The Red Tower*). The European Abstract movement is represented by Kupka, Kandinsky (*Landscape with Red Spots* and the *White Cross*), Mondrian, Van Doesburg, Malevich, Pevsner, Lissitzky and Hélion. The are works by Arp, Picabia, Schwitters, and Ernst from the Dada movement, while the fantastic elements in the works by Chagall (*The Rain*) and Klee (*Magic Garden*) link these artists to Surrealism which is well represented by Ernst (*The Kiss, Dressing the Bride, The Antipope*), Miró (*Dutch Interior II, Seated Woman II*), Magritte (*Empire of Light*), Delvaux, Dalì (*The Birth of Liquid Desires*), Tanguy, Comell, Brauner, Matta and others. The support that Peggy Guggenheim gave young American artists in the 'forties, is documented by paintings by Jackson Pollock (*The Moon Woman, Alchemistry*), young works by Motherwell, Rothko, Baziotes and Still and a large painting by Gorky. Post-war European Art is represented by Bacon, Dubuffet, Vedova, Fontana, Jorn, Appel, Nicholson, Sutherland, Bacci, Tancredi and many others. The collection also includes important sculptures: two bronzes by Brancusi (*Maiastra, Bird in Space*), works by Giacometti (*Woman Walking, Woman with Slit Throat*). The headboard from Peggy Guggenheim's bed is a unique piece by Alexander Calder.

The museum hosts many modern shows; there is also a **Museum Shop** and a **Museum Cafè** in the new wing, as well as the large, shaded garden which is open according to the museum's schedule.

## SANTA MARIA GLORIOSA DEI FRARI

This Romanesque-Gothic style Franciscan church, like its Dominican counterpart San Zanipolo, contains the tombs of a number of famous Venetians. Begun by the Francis-can monks in 1250, after

Right: *the
church of Santa
Maria Gloriosa
dei Frari.*
Opposite page:
*the church of
Santa Maria di
Nazareth.*

a design attributed to Nicola Pisano, it was later re-elaborated and enlarged by Scipione Bon in 1338, though it was not finished until 1443. The unadorned façade is divided into three sections by pilaster strips surmounted by pinnacles.

The statues over the central portal are by Alessandro Vittoria (1581). The Romanesque bell tower is the second tallest in Venice, right after St. Mark's.

### THE INTERIOR

The Latin cross interior, with aisles set off by twelve plain columns, is truly majestic in its Franciscan simplicity. The church contains funerary monuments of numerous famous Venetians of the 14th to 18th centuries, not the least of which is Titian's. Right aisle: the

first altar by Longhena has sculpture by Giusto le Court, second bay, the *tomb of Titian*, who died of plague in 1576, is a mediocre work executed by followers of Canova in 1852; third altar, sculptures by Alessandro Vittoria, among which a fine *St. Jerome*. To the right of the righthand transept is the *monument to Jacopo Marcello*, the Venetian admiral, by Pietro Lombardo. In the sacristy which looks like a beautiful miniature church is a masterpiece by Giovanni Bellini, still in its original frame, on the altar. The triptych painted in 1488 depicts the *Virgin Enthroned, Music-making Angels,* and *Saints*. In the third apse chapel is another triptych, this one by Bartolomeo Vivarini. On the altar of the first chapel is a statue of *St. John the Baptist* by Donatello. **THE CHOIR**: on the right wall is the Gothic-Renaissance *monument to*

*Doge Francesco Foscari* by the Bregno brothers (c. 1475). On the left wall, a Renaissance masterpiece, the *monument to Doge Nicolò Tron* by Antonio Rizzo (1476). Behind the main altar is Titian's celebrated altarpiece, the *Assumption of the Virgin* of 1518, regarded as one of the greatest compositional feats in art. In the first apse chapel on the left is a fine altarpiece by Bernardo Licinio (1535); in the third one, an altarpiece by Alvise Vivarini and Marco Basaiti representing *St. Ambrose Enthroned* (1503). In the fourth chapel is a triptych by Bartolomeo Vivarini on the altar and, on the baptismal font, a *statue of St. John the Baptist* by Sansovino (1554). Left aisle: over the second altar, another masterpiece by Titian, the *Pesaro Altarpiece*, depicting the *Virgin with Members of the Pesaro Family*, painted by

the master in 1526. Farther on is a huge *monument to Doge Giovanni Pesaro* by Longhena (1669), followed by the *tomb of Antonio Canova* built from a design left by the great sculptor himself.

## THE CHURCH OF SANTA MARIA DI NAZARETH

 Baldassarre Longhena was commissioned by the Barefoot (scalzi) Carmelite monks to design the church in 1670, but it was not finished until 1705, the year it was also consecrated. The façade, an outstanding example of the Venetian Baroque, was designed by Giuseppe Sardi, who drew his inspiration from Classical architecture. It consists of two tiers of twin columns framing huge niches which contain statues presumably carved by Bernardino Falcone. The whole is surmounted by a triangular tympanum adorned with sculpture. Unfortunately, one of the church's prize artworks, a fresco portraying the *Transportation from the House of Loreto*, by Giovan Battista Tiepolo, was destroyed during World War I. It has since been replaced by another fresco, the *Proclamation of the Motherhood of the Virgin at the Council of Ephesus*, by the painter Ettore Tito.

## THE INTERIOR

The elaborate decoration of the interior perfectly reflects the rich decoration of the exterior. The inside is a profusion of sculpture, gilded stucco and colored marble. The *main altar*, crowned by a canopy resting on eight marble columns, was designed by Giuseppe Pozzo in the exuberant Baroque style of the day. The statues of *St. Theresa* and *St. John of the Cross* on either side of the altar are fine works attributed to Bernardino Falcone. In the second chapel on the right is a ceiling fresco by Giovan Battista Tiepolo depicting *St. Theresa in Glory*. Another Tiepolo ceiling fresco is to be found in the first chapel on the left. It represents the *Sermon in the Garden* and the *Angel of the Passion*. In the second chapel on the left known as the Chapel of St. Carmel, is the tomb of Ludovico Manin, the last doge of the Serenissima Repubblica di San Marco who ceased being such on May 12, 1797 when the French overthrew the Republic.

## THE CHURCH OF SANTA MARIA DELLA SALUTE

 The vicissitudes throughout the construction of the church were many and varied: here we shall try to recount the most interesting ones. In 1630 Venice was struck by a terrible plague which caused thousands to perish. The Senate thus decided that, should Divine Providence intercede on the city's behalf, the citizenry would erect a huge church in honor of the Virgin. The plague ended and the Senate announced a competition for the design of the church. All of the outstanding architects of the day took part and the project was awarded to a young man, Baldassarre Longhena. Work began in 1631, but soon grave difficulties set in. First of all, the terrain was unable to support the weight of the building going up and began to give way. Longhena solved the problem by inserting a host of supporting beams deep into the soil. But his troubles were not yet over.

When the central dome was about to be set up, it looked as though the walls, would be unable to bear its weight. Longhena thought up an ingenious solution: he added a series of curlicue braces to help support the drum upon which the dome rests and which give the church its unique and dis-

*The church of Santa Maria della Salute.*

tinctive appearance. By the time the church could be consecrated in 1687, Baldassare Longhena was five years dead. Ever since, on November 21 each year, a picturesque procession, in which the whole city of Venice takes part, is held. On this occasion, a bridge connecting the church to the opposite shore is put up. The church has an octagonal plan and is surmounted by a great dome and a smaller dome directly over the choir.

## THE INTERIOR

Simple yet grandiose, the interior is shaped like an octagon over which rises the great dome. It has six side chapels. At the first right-hand altars are paintings by Luca Giordano recounting the Story of Mary: the *Presentation of Virgin at the Temple*, the *Assumption* and the *Nativity of the Virgin*. At the third altar on the left is a late work by Titian, the *Pentecost*. The marble

sculpture *Plague Fleeing Before the Virgin* on the main altar is by Giusto Le Court. Among Titian master-pieces in the sacristy are the *Death of Abel*, the *Sacrifice of Abraham*, and *David and Goliath* (1543) on the ceiling, and *St. Mark and Saints* (1512) over the altar. Tintoretto's painting, the *Wedding at Cana*, is on the wall.

# THE CHURCH OF SAN ZACCARIA

This is one of the most interesting churches in Venice. Built in the 9th century, it was altered in the 15th and 16th centuries by Antonio Gambello and Mauro Coducci. Coducci also designed the distinc-tive six-section façade, one of the foremost architectural designs to have come out of the Venetian Renaissance. The statue of *St. Zacharias* above the portal is by Alessandro Vittoria.

## THE INTERIOR

Lofty columns set off the three naves of this church which has a

Above: *the interior of the church of Santa Maria della Salute;* right: *the façade of the church of San Zaccaria.*

Gothic apse and peribolos with radiating chapels. The walls are hung with impressive paintings by the major late 17th century Venetian masters. At the second altar on the left is a famous altarpiece by Giovanni Bellini, the *Virgin and Child with Saints*, painted in 1505. From the right aisle we enter the Chapel of St. Athanasius which contains exquisite carved Gothic choir stalls (1455-1464), a *Virgin and Saints* by Palma the Elder and, over the entrance, the *Birth of St. John the Baptist* by Tintoretto. From here we enter another chapel with a polygonal apse, the Chapel of St. Tarsius. A real gem, the chapel contains important ceiling frescoes representing *God the Father and Saints* painted in 1442 by the celebrated Florentine master Andrea del Castagno and, on the walls, three magnificent altar-pieces by Giovanni d'Alemagna and Antonio Vivarini. At the end of the left aisle is the tomb, with self-portrait of the sculptor Alessandro Vittoria, who was buried here.

## THE CHURCH OF SS. GIOVANNI E PAOLO

Started by the Dominican friars in 1246, it was not finished until 1430. Like its Franciscan counterpart, Santa Maria Gloriosa dei Frari, it is an outstanding example of the architectural style known as Venetian Gothic. Inside are the mortal remains of some of the Serenissima's best-known figures. The

*The church of San Zanipolo (Sts. John and Paul).*

façade, a combination of Gothic (Byzantine sculpture) and Renaissance (the elaborate carved portal by Bartolomeo Bon), was never finished.

## THE INTERIOR

It is in the form of a Latin cross with a single aisle and a cluster of five apses. Around the doorway are three *tombs of members of the Mocenigo family*, the finest of which was built for Doge Pietro Mocenigo by Pietro Lombardo in 1485 (on the right). Starting at the first altar of the right aisle is a *Virgin and Saints* by Francesco Bissolo and at the second the *San Vincenzo Ferreri* altarpiece by Giovanni Bellini (1465). After the Chapel of Our Lady of Sorrows, which leads to the Baptistry, we come to the *Monument to the Valier Family Doges* by Andrea Tirali (18th century). At the end of the aisle is an elaborately decorated chapel, dedicated to St. Dominic, whose ceiling fresco representing *St. Dominic in Glory* is one of the masterpieces of Piazzetta (1727). In the right transept *Jesus Carrying the Cross* by Alvise Vivarini, *St. Anthony and the Poor* by Lorenzo Lotto (1542) and, by the second altar, *Christ and Saints* by Rocco Marconi. The 15th century Gothic window by Bartolomeo Vivarini is truly magnificent.

The choir conveys a majestic effect with its light-filled polygonal apse and Baroque main altar. On the right is the 14th century *Monument to Doge Michele Morosini*, with a mosaic *Crucifixion* and, a bit further on, the *monument to Doge Leonardo Loredan* of 1572. To the left are *monuments* to two other doges, *Doge Andrea Vendramin* by Pietro and Tullio Lombardo (15th century) and *Doge Marco Corner* with a statue of the *Virgin* by Nino Pisano. At the far side of the left transept is a monument to Doge Antonio Venier by the Dalle Masegnes and below it is the entrance to the 16th century Chapel of the Rosary, once adorned with sculpture by Alessandro Vittoria and paintings by Tintoretto, Bassano, and others (it unfortunately perished in a fire in 1867).

The reconstructed ceiling contains three works by Veronese: the *Annunciation*, the *Assumption, and* the *Adoration of the Shepherds*. Along the walls are 18th century sculptures and a pair of bronze *candlesticks* by Alessandro Vittoria. From the left aisle we enter the elegant Sacristy adorned with paintings by Palma the Younger. Continuing on, funerary *monuments to Doge Pasquale Malipiero* by Pietro Lombardo, *Senator Bonzi, Doge Tommaso Mocenigo* by 15th century Florentine artists, and, lastly, *Niccolò Marcello* by Pietro Lombardo. A *statue of St. Jerome* by Alessandro Vittoria adorns the first altar.

## THE CHURCH OF MADONNA DELL'ORTO

According to an old tradition, a miraculous statue of the Virgin (today preserved inside the Church) was found in the orto (garden) which originally covered this zone. The façade is an attractive mixture of the Romanesque and Gothic styles. The statues of the *Apostles* in the upper niches of the sides of the façade are by followers of the Dalle Masegnes.

## THE INTERIOR

The interior is built on a basilica plan; the aisles are offset by ten marble columns and a polygonal apse. The church contains numerous paintings by Jacopo Robusti, better known as Tintoretto, who was buried here in 1594. His tomb, marked by a simple stone plaque, is inside the church to the right of the choir. By the first altar of the right aisle is *St. John in Ecstasy with Other Saints*, the masterpiece of Cima da Conegliano (1493). Above the Chapel of St. Maurus is Tintoretto's *Presentation of the Virgin at the Temple*. The paintings in the choir (the *Last Judgement*, *Adoration of the Golden Calf*, and *Moses Receiving the Tablets of the Law*) are all by Titian who painted them when he had reached the height of his creative powers. In the fourth chapel off the left aisle is another Tintoretto, *St. Agnes Raising Licino from the Dead*. The *Virgin and Child* in the first chapel is by Giovanni Bellini.

## THE CHURCH OF SANTI APOSTOLI

This church's origins date from long ago, although it was remodeled several times until 1575 when it was radically restructured to its present form. On the Campo di Santi Apostoli is a house oddly nestled in between the bell tower and the dome of the Corner Chapel. The bell tower of 1672 was completed with a bell chamber designed by Andrea Tirali. The brick façade is not particularly noteworthy.

## THE INTERIOR

Inside the rectangular church, we first note the ceiling with frescoes of the *Glorification of the Eucharist* and the *Apostles* by Fabio Canal and G. Gaspari (1748).

The Cappella Corner on the right side was remodeled in the 16th century; its Lombard-style architecture has been attributed to Mauro Coducci. On the right wall is the *tomb of Marco Corner* attributed to Tullio Lombardo, the one on the left is the *tomb of Cardinal Giorgio Corner*. On the altar is a fine altarpiece depicting the *Communion of St. Lucy* by Giovan Battista Tiepolo and, on the altar of the next chapel, a painting of the *Nativity of the Virgin* by Giorgio Contarini. In another of the righthand chapels we can see the remains of Byzantine frescoes showing the *Deposition from the Cross* and the *Burial of Christ*. Nearby is a relief depicting *St. Sebastian*, a 16th century work by Tullio Lombardo. In the choir, on the right, is a *Last Supper* by Cesare da Conegliano (16th century) and, on the left the *Shower of Manna* by followers of Paolo Veronese.

# THE CHURCH OF THE CARMINI

S ebastiano Mariani added a Renaissance facade to this 14th century church at the beginning of the 15th century. A portal proceeded by a porch has been preserved from the original building on the left side.

The bellt ower dates from the 17th century.

## THE INTERIOR

The aisles are set off from the nave by fine 14th century columns with beautifully carved capitals.

The extensive fresco cycle of episodes from the *History of the Carmelite Order* was executed by various artists between the second half of the 17th and first half of the 18th centuries. Among the art treasures contained in the church are the altarpiece with the *Adoration of the Shepherds, Sts. Helen, Catherine,* and *Tobias and the Angel* by Cima da Conegliano (second bay of the right aisle), a relief with the *Deposition* by Francesco di Giorgio Martini (in the sacristy) and *St. Nicholas and Other Saints* by Lorenzo Lotto (second bay on the left aisle).

# THE CHURCH OF SAN BARNABA

T he church was erected between 1749 and 1776 by L. Boschetti. The simple façade, inspired by

*The church of San Barnaba.*

Classical models, consists of tall columns surmounted by a tympanum. The handsome 14th century brick bell tower has a cone-shaped cusp.

## THE INTERIOR

The interior is adorned with Corinthian columns set into the nave walls.

The ceiling was frescoed by a follower of Tiepolo's, Costantino Cedini, and shows *St. Barnabas in Glory*.

The *Birth of the Virgin* by Foler is at the first altar on the right although the most interesting works are in the choir: *St. Barnabas and Other Saints* by Damiano Mazzo on the main altar, the *Ascent to Calvary* and the *Last Supper* by Palma the Younger on the walls, and, above the altar, a painting of the *Holy Family* by Paolo Veronese.

## THE CHURCH OF THE JESUITS (GESUITI)

This grandiose church was established in the 12th century for the Order of the Cross-Bearers. It passed to the Jesuits in 1656 and was remodeled by Domenico Rossi (1715-30). The imposing Baroque façade by Fattoretto is adorned with statues of the *12 Apostles* (by F. Penso, the Groppelli brothers, and P. Baratta). The fine portal has *Angels* by Matteo Calderoni, and the *Assumption of the Virgin* in the tympanum is by G. Torretto.

*The church of the Jesuits (dei Gesuiti).*

## THE INTERIOR

The church has a Latin-cross plan and is wholly decorated with striking patterns of colored marble inlay. The stucco ceiling is by A. Stazio and the frescoes by Fontebasso. On the wall by the entrance is a *monument by G. B. Longhena* and a *bust of Priamo Da Lezze* by Jacopo Sansovino. On the first altar on the right, the *Guardian Angel* by Palma the Younger, in the second, a statue of *St. Barbara* by Morlaiter. and in the third, *Virgin and Saints* by Balestra. In the right transept is a statue of *St. Ignatius* by P. Baratta. In the chapel to the right of the main chapel is *St. Francis Xavier Preaching* by P. Liberi. The choir has elaborate architecture by Father G. Pozzo influenced by the style of Bernini, sculptures by Toretto, and frescoes by L. Dorigny. Two outstanding paintings are hanging here: the *Assumption of the Virgin* by Jacopo Tintoretto and the *Martyrdom of St. Lawrence* by Titian. In the sacristy is a painting cycle on the *theme of the Order of the Cross Bearers* executed by Palma the Younger between 1589 and 1593.

## THE CHURCH OF SAN GIOVANNI IN BRAGORA

Although its origins date back to the 8th century, the church was completely rebuilt in 1475. The strange name "Bragora" could either be derived from agora, ancient Greek for square, or "bragola" (marketplace) in Venetian dialect. The façade is one of the finest examples of the late Venetian Gothic style.

## THE INTERIOR

It has single aisles and a Gothic-style beamed ceiling. Over the entrance, *Christ before Caiaphas* by Palma the Younger. On the nave walls and the triumphal arch, are an *Annunciation, saints*, and other 15th century frescoes by a provincial artist, Tommaso di Zorzi. In the second chapel of the right aisle, an altarpiece with *St. John the Beggar*, and, in the lunette, the *Removal of the Body of St. John to Venice* by Jacopo Marieschi (the mortal remains of the saint are in an urn beneath the altar). At the end of the right aisle over the sacristy door is a painting of *Christ Blessing* by Alvise Vivarini (1493). The Renaissance choir was built by Sebastiano Mariani between 1485 and 1488. On the pillars by the entrance are two works by Vivarini, *St. Helen and Constantine by the Cross* on the right and *Christ Resurrected* on the left. On the main altar are three sculptures: *Faith* by Antonio Gai, *St. John the Evangelist*, and *St. John the Beggar* by Giovanni Marchiori. In the apse is a fine *Baptism of Christ* by Cima da Conegliano. On the walls are the *Last Supper* by Paris Bordone and the *Washing of the Feet* by Palma the Younger. In the left aisle, in the chapel closest to the choir, are two noteworthy altarpieces: a triptych representing the *Virgin Between Sts. Andrew and John the Baptist*, by Bartolomeo Vivarini on the right and *Sts. Andrew, Jerome, and Martin* on the left.

# THE CHURCH OF ST. GIORGIO MAGGIORE

The church's white façade contrasts sharply with the ochre-hued buildings around. One of Palladio's finest designs (the architect worked on the project between 1565 and 1580), the basilica was finished in 1610 by Scamozzi on the master's original plans. The façade, divided into three sections by four columns with Corinthian capitals, once more reveals Palladio's distinctive style. Statues of *Sts George and Stephen* are set between the columns with busts of the *Doges Tribuno Mommo and P. Zini* by Giulio Moro at the outer sides. The bell tower was built by Benedetto Buratti in 1791 to replace the one which collapsed in 1773. There is an unforgettable view of the city and lagoon from its top.

# THE INTERIOR

Unadorned yet imposing, the church is in the shape of an inverted Latin cross. In the second altar on the right is a wooden *Crucifix* by the great Florentine artist, Michelozzo. On the main altar of the choir is a superb bronze group by Girolamo Campagna (1593). Two great Tintorettos are hanging on the walls: the *Last Supper* on the right and the *Shower of Manna* on the left.

# SANTA MARIA FORMOSA

The much earlier church of Santa Maria Formosa was rebuilt by Mauro Coducci in 1492. It has two 16th century façades and a 17th century Baroque belfry.

*View of the Island of San Giorgio.*

## THE INTERIOR

The Latin cross interior has no aisles. The triptych in the first chapel on the right by Bartolomeo Vivarini depicts the *Nativity of the Virgin*, the *Virgin of Mercy*, and the *Meeting of Joachim and St. Anne*. The altarpiece in the right transept

with *St. Barbara and Four Saints* is by Palma the Elder (1509).

## THE CHURCH OF SANTA MARIA DEI MIRACOLI

Pietro Lombardo designed this Renaissance church in 1481. Its unusual and very attractive façade sports marble decoration over the two storey central portal surmounted by two huge windows.

## THE INTERIOR

The walls of the rectangular church are lined in precious marble and the coffered ceiling is divided into 50 lacunars with heads of *Prophets* and *Saints* by Pier Maria Pennacchi (1528). The raised choir, a masterpiece of decorative art created by the Lombardo brothers, is reached by

Preceding page: *the church of Santa Maria dei Miracoli*; below: *the church of Santa Maria Formosa*; left: *the church of San Moisè*.

an elegant staircase. The main altar is surmounted by a dome.

## THE CHURCH OF SAN MOISÈ

There has been a church on this spot since the 8th century A.D. In the 10th century the original structure was rebuilt by a certain Moise Venier who dedicated it to his own name-saint, St. Moise. Later, in the 14th century, the lovely bell tower with its distinctive brick spire was raised alongside it. The Baroque façade was designed in the second half of the 17th century by Alessandro Tremignon for Vincenzo Fini whose bust can be seen on the obelisk above the central portal (although Tremignon commissioned the sculptor Enrico Meyring with the actual execution of the decorative scheme). Many of the sculptures had to be removed during the 19th century, since they were in danger of toppling, which means that the decoration which today appears exaggeratedly ornate, was even more so in the original version.

### THE INTERIOR

The ceiling of the church is frescoed with the *Vision of Moses* by Niccolo Bambini. The first altar on the right is adorned with an 18th century marble *Pietà* by Antonio Corradini and a painting in the Caraccis' style representing the *Adoration of the Magi* by Giuseppe

Diamantini. Also on the right is a fine *pulpit* carved in the 18th century by Tagliapietra. In the second altar is the *Invention of the Cross* by Pietro Liberi. In the sacristy is a bronze altar frontal with a *Deposition* scene, by the 17th century Genoese artists, Niccolò and Sebastiano Roccatagliata. The main altar of the church is an elaborate Baroque creation by Tremignon decorated with sculptures by Meyring. In the choir are 16th century carved wooden choir stalls. The left chapel contains two especially noteworthy works, the *Last Supper* by Palma the Younger and the *Washing of the Feet*, a late work by Jacopo Tintoretto.

## THE CHURCH OF SAN POLO

According to tradition the church was founded in 837 by Doge Pietro Gradonico. It was then rebuilt in the Gothic style and remodeled many times throughout the centuries. Its lovely bell tower dates from 1362.

## THE INTERIOR

It is in the form of a basilica with single aisles. On the inside façade are two fine works, the *Communion of the Apostles* by Jacopo Tintoretto and the *Baptism of Constantine* by Piazza. Over the first altar on the right is the *Assumption of the Virgin* by Jacopo Tintoretto. In the Chapel of the Blessed Sacrament built in the Lombard style are four paintings by Giuseppe Salviati recounting *Episodes from the Life of Christ*. In the choir are paintings by Palma the Younger whose subjects are: the *Temptation and Liberation of St. Anthony, the Conversion of St. Paul, the Giving of the Keys to St. Peter*, and *St. Mark Preaching*. In addition, there are two paintings by G. B. Tiepolo representing *Angels in Glory* and the *Via Crucis*. On the main altar, between bronze statues of *St. Paul* and *St. Anthony Abbot* by Vittoria, is a 15th century painted *Crucifix*. The chapel to the left of the main chapel contains a *Visitation* by Veronese. At the second altar on the left is the *Virgin with St. John Nepomucenus* by G. B. Tiepolo.

*Campo San Polo.*

# THE CHURCH OF IL REDENTORE

The church is the result of Andrea Palladio's architectural genius combined with the technical skill of Antonio Da Ponte who built it between 1577 and 1592. It was put up in thanksgiving for the cessation of another of the innumerable plague epidemics which had taken its toll of Venetian victims. A huge staircase leads up to a façade proper which consists of a single order of columns surmounted by a tympanum. Crowning the church is a dome flanked by a pair of bell towers.

## THE INTERIOR

The inside reflects the classical harmony of the outside. The stately colonnade along the interior confers a majestic effect to the whole. The Baroque main altar is adorned with bronzes by Campagna. In the sacristy are some interesting works, including a *Virgin and Child* by Alvise Vivarini, a *Baptism of Christ* by a follower of Veronese, a *Virgin and Child with Saints* by Palma the Younger, and several works by Bassano.

## THE CHURCH OF SAN SALVADOR

Although this is one of the oldest churches in Venice, it has been remodeled over the centuries, first in the 16th century by Giorgio Spavento, then by Tullio Lombardo, and lastly by Sansovino and Scamozzi, who gave it its present appearance. The intricate carved Baroque façade was designed in 1663 by Bernardino Falcone.

## THE INTERIOR

Not only one of the finest extant examples of Venetian Renaissance architecture this single-naved church is also filled with masterpieces of art. Between the second and third altars of the right aisle is the *tomb monument to Doge Francesco Venier* with *statues of Charity* and *Hope* by Sansovino. A grandiose painting of the *Annunciation* by Titian (1566) adorns the third altar. The main altar contains an embossed silver altar frontal, a superb example of 14th century Venetian craftsmanship. It is surmounted by a *Transfiguration* by Titian. In the chapel to the left of the main chapel is the *Supper at Emmaus*, recently attributed to Giovanni Bellini. In the left hand transept is a *monument to the Correr family* by Bernardo Contino.

*The church of Il Redentore.*

# THE CHURCH OF SAN SEBASTIANO

The church was built in the 1500s by an architect from Cremona, Francesco da Castiglione, who was helped by Scarpagnino. It was restored in 1867. Inside is the finest collection of Veronese's paintings to be found anywhere in Venice. (Veronese himself was buried in the church in 1588).

## THE INTERIOR

The decoration of this church was commissioned from Paolo Veronese whose exuberant youth and vigor are plainly visible. Unfortunately Veronese was confined to a wall space that hardly lent itself to fresco painting so he had to overcome difficult technical problems relating to poor lighting and tight spaces. The most noteworthy paintings are the *Story of Esther* in the ceiling panels, the *Virgin with St. Sebastian and Other Saints* by the altar of the main chapel, the *Martyrdom of Sts. Mark and Marcellinus* on the left, the *Martyrdom of St. Sebastian* on the right, and the *Annunciation* on the triumphal arch. In the chapel to the left of the main chapel are a bust of Veronese and, on the ground, his tomb slab, as well as an *organ* with panels decorated by the great master. The sacristy contains paintings by various followers of Veronese and, on the ceiling, five panels which were the first works the great artist from Verona did in Venice. After the third altar on the right is a grandiose *monument to Bishop Livio Podocataro* executed by Sansovino in 1556.

# THE CHURCH OF SAN TROVASO

This is Venetian dialect for Gervasio and Protasio, names of two important saints. Already in existence by the 11th century, the church was burnt to the ground and rebuilt in the Palladian neo-Classical style in 1583.

## THE INTERIOR

The interior has a huge choir and side chapels. At the third altar on the right is *St. Francis de Paul, Faith and Charity*, by Alvise di Friso. On the wall nearby is a *Virgin and Child* by a follower of Giovanni Bellini. In the right transept is a lovely altar frontal, a Renaissance relief attributed to Pietro Lombardo which portrays *Angels with the Symbols of the Passion*. In the chapel to the right of the main chapel is a *Crucifixion* by Domenico Tintoretto on the altar. A Gothic masterpiece, *St. Chrysogonus on Horseback* adorns the walls. It has been attributed by some to Jacobello del Fiore and by others to Michele Giambono. The choir contains the *Adoration of the Magi* and *Joachim Expelled from the Temple* by Jacopo Tintoretto and his pupils. In the chapel to the left of the main chapel is a *Temptation of St. Anthony* by Jacopo Tintoretto. The **sacristy** contains a *Virgin* by Rosalba Carriera and *Sts. John and Mary Magdalene* attributed to Tintoretto. In the **Chapel of the Blessed Sacrament** in the left transept are paintings by Tintoretto (the *Last Supper* and the *Washing of the Feet*).

*The Lido of Venice.*

We shall now turn to the group of splendid islands which are like gemstones laid out amidst the lagoon, the most precious of which is Venice herself. There are all kinds, ranging in size from tiny uninhabited islets to good-sized islands, now sleepy fishing villages, but once thriving cities.

An excursion to Torcello, Burano, and Murano is a must for those who would like to really know Venice. These island towns are fascinating not only for the art treasures they possess, but also for their hauntingly beautiful landscapes in an atmosphere of magical silence and this is not all the lagoon has to offer. We must not forget the local handicrafts; glassblowing, lacemaking, and coppercrafting are some of the typical ones practiced by the local artisans.

## THE LIDO OF VENICE

The Lido is actually an elongated island about a mile from Venice, bordered by a considerable stretch of sandy beach. Once the city's natural defense, it is now a celebrated resort. The Lido's international reputation comes from its superbly equipped hotels and excellent tourist accommodations, its fine beach, and the cultural, artistic, and sports events held here throughout the year, with the greatest concentration, of course, in summer.

From the smart sophistication of the Lido with its elegant hotels and bathing establishments, we pass to the enchanting peace of the mysterious **Isle of San Lazzaro degli Armeni**. Here a community of Armenian monks has been thriving for centuries, immersed in the silence of their convent, surrounded by luxuriant vegetation. The atmosphere of the island is permeated with memories of Byron who spent lengthy periods of his life on San Lazzaro. Sailing towards Murano we encounter the Island of **San Michele in Isola** where, according to legend, St. Romualdo, founder of the Camaldolese Order once lived (although the order held on to the island until the 19th century, today it is just a sleepy cemetery marked by majestic cypresses). Proceeding toward Burano and Torcello we encounter, on the left, the solitary Islet of **San Giacomo in Palude** and, on the right, the lovely Islet of **San Francesco del Deserto**, where solitude and silence reign over the thick vegetation surrounding the hermitage. We shall now take a closer look at the major lagoon centers, Murano with its glass factories, Burano with its lacemaking, and the former rival of Venice, Torcello.

## MURANO

Less than a mile away from Venice, Murano is a typical lagoon town spread over five islets. It is renowned for its glassblowing industry which dates back to the 13th century. The **Glass Museum** in the **Palazzo Giustiniani** exhibits rare pieces of the glassblower's art, including Roman and Egyptian objects, dating from Antiquity to the 18th century.

## THE CHURCH OF SANTI MARIA E DONATO

The church originally on the site was rebuilt in the 12th century. It is a unique example of the Venetian-Byzantine style with its hexagonal apse and double

*Bird's-eye view of the Island of Murano.*

*Church of Santa Maria e Donato.*

tier of columns creating a graceful pattern of niches and loggias.

## THE INTERIOR

The church has a basilican plan and aisles set off from the nave by ten marble columns with superb Corinthian capitals. The marble flooring dates from the 12th century. At the beginning of the left-wall is a large painted carved altarpiece which is an outstanding example of 14th century Venetian art. The mosaic showing the *Virgin in Prayer Against a Gold Ground* in the semi-dome of the apse dates from the 12th century.

## THE CHURCH OF SAN PIETRO MARTIRE

Inside this 14th century church are numerous works of art. Three of the finest are Giovanni Bellini's *Virgin Enthroned with Two Angels and Saints* and *Assumption of the Virgin and Saints*, and Veronese's *St. Jerome in the Desert* over the sacristy door.

## BURANO

Burano (originally Burianum or Boreanum) occupies four tiny islands inhabited mainly by fish-

*A typical rio on the Island of Burano.*

ermen. It was first settled in the 5th-6th centuries by refugees from Altinum fleeing Attila's fearful Huns. Though it is mostly famous for the traditional art of lacemaking which the women of the town have been handing down to their daughters for centuries, Burano also boasts noteworthy artistic treasures.

Taking the main road of the village named after its best-known native son, the 18th century composer Baldassarre Galuppi, known as "Il Suranello," we soon reach the main square and the 16th century **church of San Martino**.

Alongside is its eighteenth century bell tower which, like the Tower of Pisa, leans dangerously to one side, and the **chapel of Santa Barbara** which contains works of great interest, such as Tiepolo's huge *Crucifixion* (dated c. 1725), *St. Mark and Other Saints* by Girolamo da Santa-

croce, and several canvases by Giovanni Mansueti (end of the 16th century).

On the same square stands the **Palazzo della Podestà**, a 19th century building now occupied by the **Lacemaking School**, which was founded in 1872 so that this traditional art would never be lost.

## TORCELLO

Only six miles from Venice is one of the most fascinating spots in the lagoon. Now just a solitary village on a lonely island, it was once a flourishing hub of culture and commerce whose greatness dimmed as Venice's grew. All that is left of its long ago splendor is a group of monuments facing out on a picturesque grassy square around the so-called "caregon", which, if popu-

*Bird's eye view of the Island of Torcello.*

lar tradition is to be believed, was originally Attila's throne.

## THE CATHEDRAL

**D**edicated to St. Maria Assunta, the Cathedral's origins go back to the year 639, although it was rebuilt in the early 11th century together with its majestic bell tower. Ruins of a circular-plan 8th century baptistry are visible in front of the building.

### THE INTERIOR

Austere and simple, the church has aisles set off from the nave by columns. The inner façade is entirely covered with remarkable 12th-13th century Byzantine mosaics portraying the *Last Judgment*. In the nave are two pulpits and an iconostasis (rood screen) with exquisite transennae supporting a series of 15th century icons. In the triumphal arch is a 12th century mosaic representing the *12 Apostles* and, in the semi-dome, one of the *Virgin and Child* dating from the 13th century.

## THE CHURCH OF SANTA FOSCA

**T**he church, built around the 11th century, has an unusual octagonal shape. On the outside a portico resting on arches runs around five sides of the building, while the simple Greek cross interior has columns decorated with Byzantine capitals.

On the square, are two Gothic buildings, the **Palazzo del Consiglio** and the **Palazzo dell'Archivio**. They contain a fascinating collection of archeological finds discovered on the lagoon islands, mainly Torcello.

*The bell tower of Santa Maria Assunta.*

*The church of Santa Fosca.*

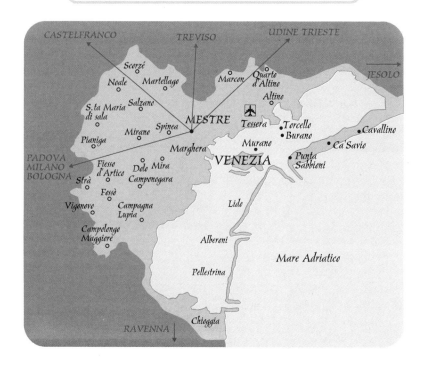

### BY CAR
From the **west** or **east**: **A4** Highway (Turin-Milan-Trieste).
From the **south**: **A13** Highway to Padua, then **A4**.
From the **north**: **A27** Highway (Vittorio Veneto Mestre).

### BY PLANE
The Marco Polo airport is located 13 km from Venice, with daily service to the main Italian and Euroepan cities.
Charter flight service is also available.

### BY MOTORBOAT
One hour trip to Piazza San Marco. ☎ 5222303

### BY BUS
Bus **n.5**; airport shuttle, hourly arrivals in Piazzale Roma.

### BY MOTORBOAT-TAXI
The trip is faster, but definitely more expensive.

### BY TRAIN
Venice is connected to Milan, Trieste, Bologna, Pordenone, and all of Europe.

**PUBLIC TRANSPORTATION**
Piazzale Roma
☎ 5287886
**TRAINS:**
Stazione Santa Lucia e
Stazione di Mestre
☎ 715555
**AIRLINES:**
Aeroporto Marco Polo
☎ 661262
**TAXIS:**
Radio Taxi
☎ 936222
**BYCICLE RENTAL:**
Bruno Lazzari
Gran viale Santa Maria
Elisabetta,
Lido, 21b
☎ 5268019
Giorgio Barbieri
Via Zara, Lido 5
☎ 5261490
**GARAGES:**
Venezia, Isola del Tronchetto
☎ 5207555
Venezia, P.le Roma
Garage Comunale
☎ 5222308
Venezia, P.le Roma
Garage S. Marco
☎ 5232213
**PARKING:**
Venezia, Isola del Tronchetto
☎ 5207555
Venezia, P.le Roma ACI
☎ 5206235
Punta Sabbioni
Treporti Ricevitoria
Turistic Ass. Information (I.A.T)
Venezia S. Marco
☎ 5226356
Lido, Viale S. M Elisabetta
☎ 52665721
Marghera, Rotatoria autostradale

☎ and Fax 937764
Cà Savio, via Fausta, 79/G
☎ and Fax 966010
Dolo - Arino Sud
Autostrada Padova - Venezia
☎ 413945

## EMERGENCY PHONE NUMBERS

☎

PoliEmergency........................113
**Police:**
Santa Chiara.................**5284666**
**Carabinieri:**
Emergency............................112
**Carabinieri:**
Piazzale Roma.............**52352333**
**Ambulance:**
Venezia..........................**5230000**
**Volunteer Ambulance.....914186**
ACI (Automobile Club-road
service)....................................116
**Harbor Office.................5205600**
**Police Headquarters and**
**Passport Office..............2703511**
**Marco Polo Airport.......2606111**
**Airport:**
Information....................**2609260**
**Airport:**
Lost & Found.................**2606436**
**Fire Department:**
Venezia..........................**5200222**
**Municipal Police:**
Venezia..........................**2708203**
**Municipal Police:** Piazzale
Roma/Tronchetto.........**5222612**
**Italian State Railways:**
Information.....................**715555**
**Italian State Railways:**
Lost & Found...................**785238**
**City Hall........................2708111**
**Tourist Information**
**Office................................5226356**

## BANKS

Banca Commerciale Italiana
☎ 5296811

Banca del Friuli
☎ 5285744

Banca d'Italia
☎ 2709111

Banca di Roma
☎ 662411

Banca Nazionale del Lavoro
☎ 667511

Banca Naz. delle Comunicazioni
☎ 717722

Banca Popolare di Novara
☎ 5231640

Banca Popolare di Verona
☎ 5205344

Banco Ambrosiano Veneto
☎ 2903111

Banco di Napoli
☎ 5209855

Banco di Sicilia
☎ 5220525

Banco San Marco
☎ 5293711

Cassa di Risparmio di Venezia
☎ 5291111

Cassa di Risp. Province Lombarde
☎ 5330411

Credito Italiano
☎ 5226330

Deutsche Bank
☎ 5490811

Istituto Federale Casse Risparmio
☎ 5205111

Istituto Mobiliare Italiano
☎ 5229403

Mediocredito delle Venezie
☎ 5218444

Monte dei Paschi di Siena
☎ 5204000

## CONSULATES

**Austria**
Santa Croce 252
☎ 5240556
**Belgium**
San Marco 1470
☎ 5224124
**Brazil**
Campo S. Luca
4580/A
☎ 5204131
**Chile**
San Marco 286
☎ 5202442
**Repubblica
Ceca**
S. Marco 1583/A
☎ 5210383
**Denmark**
San Marco 4020
☎ 5200822

**Finland**
S. Giuliano, Mestre
☎ 5319066
**France**
Dorsoduro 1397
☎ 5222392
**Germany**
Cannaregio
4201
☎ 5237675
**Great Britain**
Dorsoduro 1051
☎ 5227207
**Greece**
S. Polo, Rialto 720
☎ 5237260
**Hungary**
San Marco 286
☎ 5239408
**Liberia**
V. Istria - Lido
☎ 5265878

**Luxembourg**
Castello 5312
☎ 5222047
**Malta**
Santa Croce 515
☎ 5222644
**Mexico**
San Marco 286
☎ 5237445
**Netherlands**
San Marco 423
☎ 5283416
**Norway**
Rotonda Garibaldi
12/7 - Mestre
☎ 5340447
**Panama**
S. Maria Elisabetta
8/A - Lido
☎ 5267169
**Portugal**
San Marco 1253
☎ 5223446

**Rep. S. Marino**
S. Marco 5017/A
☎ 5228239
**Republic of
South Africa**
Santa Croce 464
☎ 5241599
**Sweden**
c/o Ligabue s.p.a.
Piazzale Roma -
Santa Croce 499
☎ 2705611
**Switzerland**
Dorsoduro 810
☎ 5225996
**Turkey**
San Marco 2414
☎ 5230707
**United States
of America**
Largo Donegani
1, Milano
☎ 02/290351

# HOSTELS IN VENICE

| | ROOMS | BEDS | TOILETS | BREAKFAST | LUNCH | DINNER |
|---|---|---|---|---|---|---|
| **Ostello di Venezia**<br>Giudecca 86 ☎ 5238211<br>Closed from 16 January to 1 February | 60 | 273 | 54 | yes | yes | yes |
| **Istituto Canossiano**<br>Ponte Piccolo 428 ☎ 5222157<br>Giudecca - open all year | 2 | 35 | 7 | no | no | no |
| **Domus Cavanis**<br>Dorsoduro 912 ☎ 522826<br>Open from 15 June to 15 September | 18 | 25 | 8 | yes | no | no |

# AGRITOURISM ESTABLISHMENTS

**Enzo Gelsomina- Mayer**
via del Marinaio, 4 - Cavallino
Open from 1 April to 30 September
☎ 5370431

**La Fenice - Serafini Mario**
Via Orlanda, 6 - Mestre
☎ 5420161

**Le Garzette - Orazio Renza**
Via Malamocco, 32 - Lido di Venezia
Open from 5 January to 30 November
☎ 731078

**Zanella Gabriella**
Via Forti, 16 - Sant' Erasmo
Open all year
☎ 5285329

**Le Manciane - Vianello Galdino**
Via Lio Piccolo, 29 - Cavallino
Open all year
☎ 658977

# CAMPSITES IN VENICE

**** **Camping Alba d'Oro,** Via Triestina, 214/B - Località Ca' Noghera
*Restaurant - Market - Espresso Bar Swimming Pool - Children's play area.*
☎ 5415102

** **Campeggio Fusina,** Via Moranzani, 79/bis - Località Fusina -Malcontenta
*Market - Espresso Bar - Bazaar - Barber - Volley Ball - Boat Rental - Children's play area - Restaurant - Photographer Table Tennis - Currency Exchange.*
☎ 5470064 - **Fax** 5470050

** **Campeggio Venezia,** Via Orlanda, 8 Località Campalto - Mestre
*Restaurant - Market - Espresso Bar.*
☎ 975928

* **Campeggio Marco Polo,** Via Triestina, 164 - Località Tessera
*Restaurant - Market - Espresso Bar Children's play area - Game room*
☎ 5415346

* **Camping Jolly,** Via A. De Marchi, 7 Località Marghera
*Market - Espresso Bar - Bazaar Swimming Pool - Canteen - Children's play area - Game room - Table Tennis Soccer Field - Snack Bar - Restaurant*
☎ and **Fax** 920312

* **Camping Rialto,** Via Orlanda, 16 Località Mestre
*Market - Espresso Bar*
☎ 900785

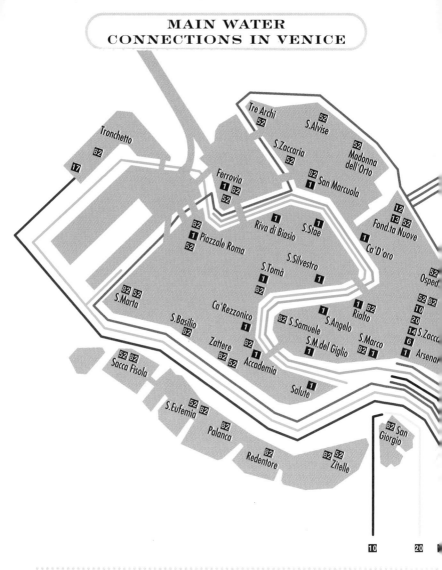

The most widely used vaporetto lines are: 1, 2, 5 and 12.

There are three types of vessels:

**VAPORETTO:** which is slow and makes every stop along the Grand Canal.

**MOTOSCAFO:** which is faster and makes fewer stops along its route.

**MOTONAVE:** which is a big ferry and covers the longer routes.

**FARES:** Tickets must be purchased before boarding. A standard ticket is valid for 90 minutes. There is a full-day ticket that can be used on all routes except 2 and 28. Holders of "youth cards" issued by the city of Venice can obtain less expensive passes.

There are also cards for congress participants; they are valid for eight days and entitle the holders to discounts on all routes except 2.

From the automobile terminal at Tronchetto to the historic city center:
**Line 82** via the Grand Canal (for the railroad station, Rialto, S. Marco) or via Canale della Giudecca (direct to S. Marco), in summer it continues to the Lido.
**Line 3**: summer line, morning service only to Rialto and S. Marco.
From Piazzale Roma, **Line 1**: makes all stops along the Grand Canal to the Lido, or **Line 82**.
From S. Marco to return to the railroad station, Piazzale Roma and Tronchetto, **Line 4** (summertime, afternoon service only), or **Line 82**.
From Venice to the Lido, we suggest motorboat **Line 6** from the Paglia station (between S. Zaccaria and S. Marco); it departs every 20 minutes, the trip takes fifteen minutes.
The Lido can also be reached by car, using the ferry boat from Tronchetto (the trip takes about 35 minutes).
To go to Burano and Torcello: **Line 14** from S. Zaccaria (about 1 hour and 15 minutes), or **Line 12** from Fondamente Nove (about 45 minutes).
**Line 52** goes to Fondamente Nove from Piazzale Roma or from the railroad station, and then continues to Murano.
From the Jesolo shore, it is best to reach Venice from Punta Sabbioni, where a motorboat takes about 45 minutes. Burano and Torcello can be reached by motorboat in a half hour.
The automobile terminal at Fusina is in service during the summer, with **Line 16** departures for Venice (Zattere) every half hour during the season.
Detailed and updated information and routes and schedules can be obtained form the Centro Informazioni ed Accoglienza della Azienda di Transporti ACTV in Piazzale Roma, open daily, including holidays, from 7:30 a.m. to 8:00 p.m. (phone 041-5287886 - fax 041-5222633).
It is advisable to purchase round-trip tickets, or special 24 hour, 3 or 7 day tickets.

The **Carta Venezia** is valid for three years, and entitles the holder to discounts ranging from 50% to 60% on all public transportation. An ID photo and identification are needed to obtain the Carta Venezia.
For information about public transportation in Venice, contact:
ACTV DI PIAZZALE ROMA (PHONE 5287886)
SAN MARCO (PHONE 780310)
MESTRE (PHONE 972073)


The line 1, 2 and 5 vaporetti go to nearly everywhere in the city, even along the Grand Canal.

# HOTELS

***** L

**Cipriani,** Giudecca 10 (central location) ☎ 5207744
**Danieli,** Riva degli Schiavoni 4196 (panoramic) ☎ 5226480
**Gritti Palace,** San Marco 2467 ☎ 794611

****

**Amadeus,** Lista di Spagna 227 (central location) ☎ 715300
**Bauer Grunwald & Grand Hotel,** S. Marco 1459 C. S. Moisè ☎ 5207022
**Bellini,** Cannaregio 116 (central location) ☎ 715095
**Carlton Executive,** Santa Croce 578 (central location) ☎ 718488
**Cavalletto & Doge Orseolo,** S. Marco 1107 (central location) ☎ 5200955
**Concordia,** Calle Larga - San Marco 367 ☎ 5206866
**Europa & Regina,** San Marco 2159 ☎ 5200477
**Gabrielli Sandwirth** Riva degli Schiavoni 4110 ☎ 5231580
**Londra Palace,** Riva degli Schiavoni 4171 (central location) ☎ 5200533
**Luna Hotel Baglioni,** San Marco 1243 (central location) ☎ 5289840
**Metropole,** Riva degli Schiavoni 4149 (central location) ☎ 5205044
**Monaco & Gran Canal,** San Marco 1325 ☎ 5200211
**Palazzo del Giglio,** San Marco 2462 ☎ 5205166
**Principe,** Lista di Spagna 146/7 (central location) ☎ 715022
**Sofitel,** Santa Croce 245 (central location) ☎ 710400
**Star Hotel Splendid Suisse,** Mercerie 760 ☎ 5200755

***

**Abbazia,** Calle Priuli, 68 - Cannaregio (100m from station) ☎ 717333
**Accademia Villa Maravege,** Dorsoduro 1058 (central loc.) ☎ 5210188
**Al Sole,** Santa Croce 136 (central location) ☎ 5232144
**American,** San Vio - Accademia 628 (central location) ☎ 5204733
**Ateneo,** San Marco 1876 (central location) ☎ 5200777
**Basilea,** Santa Croce 817 (central location) ☎ 718477
**Bonvecchiati,** Calle Goldoni 4488 - S. Marco (central loc.) ☎ 5285017
**Carpaccio,** San Polo 2765 (on Canal Grande) ☎ 5235946
**Castello,** Castello 4365 (central location) ☎ 5230217
**Do Pozzi,** San Marco 2347 (central location) ☎ 5207855
**Firenze,** San Marco 1490 (central location) ☎ 5222858
**Gardena,** Santa Croce 239 (central location) ☎ 5235549
**Kette,** San Moisè 2053 - San Marco (central location) ☎ 5207766
**La Fenice et des Artistes,** S. Marco 1936 (central location) ☎ 5232333
**Marconi,** San Polo Riva del Vin 729 (central location) ☎ 5222068
**Nazionale,** Cannaregio 158 (central location) ☎ 716133
**Olimpia,** Santa Croce 395 (central location) ☎ 5226141
**Panada,** Calle degli Specchieri 656 - San Marco ☎ 5209088
**Piccola Fenice,** San Marco 3614 ☎ 5204909
**San Moisè,** San Marco 2058 (central location) ☎ 5203755
**Scandinavia,** Castello 5240 (central location) ☎ 5223507

# HOTELS

**

Ai Due Fanali, Santa Croce 946 (central location)  ☎ 718490
Atlantico, Calle dei Rimedi 4416 - Castello  ☎ 5209244
Campiello, San Zaccaria 4647 (central location)  ☎ 5205764
Casa Fontana, Campo San Zaccaria 4701
Castello (central location)  ☎ 5220579
Dolomiti, Calle Priuli 73  ☎ 715113
Falier, Salizzada S. Pantalon 130 (central location)  ☎ 710882
Gallini, Calle della Verona 3673 - San Marco  ☎ 5204515
Gorizia, Calle dei Fabbri 4696/A (central location)  ☎ 5223737
Hesperia, Cannaregio 459 (central location)  ☎ 715251
La Calcina, Dorsoduro 780 (central location)  ☎ 5206466
La Forcola, Cannaregio 2356 (50m fromCasinò)  ☎ 5241484
Lisbona, San Marco 2153 (central location)  ☎ 5286774
Messner, Dorsoduro 216 (central location)  ☎ 5227443
Mignon, Cannaregio 4535 (central location)  ☎ 5237388
Orion, San Marco Spadaria 700/A (central location)  ☎ 5223053
Paganelli, Riva degli Schiavoni 4182 (central location)  ☎ 52243
San Zulian, San Marco 535 (central location)  ☎ 5225872
Serenissima, Calle Goldoni - San Marco 4486 (central loc.)  ☎ 5200011
Stella Alpina Edelweiss, Calle Priuli
Cannaregio 99/D (central location)  ☎ 715179
Trovatore, Calle delle Rasse 4534 (central location)  ☎ 5224611

*

Al Gallo, Santa Croce 197/G (central location)  ☎ 5236761
Al Gazzettino, San Marco 4971 (central location)  ☎ 5286523
Antico Capon, Dorsoduro 3004/B (central location)  ☎ 5285292
Bridge, Castello 4498 (central location)  ☎ 5205287
Budapest, San Marco 2143  ☎ 5220514
Casa Boccassini, Cannaregio 5295  ☎ 5229892
Casa Peron, Salizzada San Pantalon 85 (central location)  ☎ 711038
Corona, Castello 4464  ☎ 5229174
Da Pino, Dorsoduro 3941 (central location)  ☎ 5223646
Doni, Castello S. Zaccaria 4656 (at S. Marco)  ☎ 5224267
Galleria, Accademia 878/A  ☎ 5204172
Locanda Fiorita, San Marco 3457/A (central location)  ☎ 5234754
Minerva e Nettuno, Lista di Spagna 230  ☎ 715968
Piave, Castello 4838/40 (central location)  ☎ 5285174
Riva, Castello Ponte dell'Angelo 5310  ☎ 5227034
San Geremia, Cannaregio 290/A (central location)  ☎ 716260
San Salvador, Calle Galiazzo 5264  ☎ 5289147
Santa Lucia, Cannaregio 358  ☎ 715180
Tiepolo, Castello 4510  ☎ 5231315
Villa Rosa, Calle della Misericordia 389 - Cannaregio  ☎ 716569

## RESTAURANTS

**A la Valigia**, Calle dei Fabbri 4697 (central location) ☎ 5223737
Typical setting - home cooking

**A la Vecia Cavana**, SS. Apostoli 4624 - Cannaregio ☎ 5287106
(central location) Family setting - typical cuisine

**Agli Alboretti**, Dorsoduro 882 (central location) ☎ 5230058
Elegant setting - refined cuisine

**Al Campiello**, Calle dei Fuseri 4346 (central location) ☎ 5206396
Elegant setting - refined cuisine

**Al Conte Pescaor**, San Marco 544 (central location) ☎ 5221483
Typical setting - local cuisine

**Al Giardinetto**, Castello 2375 (central location) ☎ 5285332
Typical setting - local cuisine

**Antico Martini**, San Marco 1983 - (c/o Teatro la Fenice) ☎ 5224121
Elegant setting - refined cuisine

**Canova**, San Marco 1243 (central location) ☎ 5209550
Elegant setting - refined cuisine

**Da Crecola**, Santa Croce 1459 (central location) ☎ 5241496
Family setting - home cooking

**Do Leoni**, Riva degli Schiavoni 4171 (central location) ☎ 5200533
Elegant setting - local cuisine

**Gran Caffè Quadri**, Piazza San Marco 120 ☎ 5222105
Elegant setting - refined cuisine

**Hostaria da Franz**, Castello 754 ☎ 5227505
Typical setting - local cuisine

**Il Cortile**, Calle XXII Marzo 2398 ☎ 5208938
Elegant setting - local cuisine

**La Terrazza**, Riva degli Schiavoni 4196 ☎ 5226480
(panoramic) Elegant setting - local cuisine

**Les Deux Lion**, Riva degli Schiavoni 4171 (central location) ☎ 5220533
Refined cuisine

**Linea d'Ombra**, Dorsoduro Punta Dogana 19 (central location) ☎ 5204720
Typical setting - local cuisine

**Malamocco**, Castello 4650 - San Zaccaria (central location) ☎ 5227438
Typical setting - local cuisine

**Martini Scala**, San Marco 1980 (central location) ☎ 5224121
Elegant setting - refined cuisine

**Osteria ai Schiavoni**, Calle del Doge 4734 (central location) ☎ 5226763
Typical setting - local cuisine

**Papageno**, Cannaregio 225/226 (central location) ☎ 715610
Elegant setting - local cuisine

**Paradiso Perduto**, Cannaregio 2540 - Fond. Misericordia ☎ 720851
Typical setting - local cuisine

**Riviera**, Dorsoduro 1473 Zattere - Canale della Giudecca ☎ 5227621
Family setting - local cuisine

**Taverna al Pozzo**, San Marco 1016 (central location) ☎ 5223649
Family setting - home cooking

**Taverna Capitan Uncino**, Santa Croce 1501 ☎ 721901
Typical setting - local cuisine

## RESTAURANTS

**Trattoria San Tomà,** S. Paolo 2864/A - Campo San Tomà ☎ 5238819
(centro storico) Typical setting - local cuisine
**Vino Vino,** Ponte delle Veste 2007/A (c/o Teatro la Fenice) ☎ 5237027
Family setting - local cuisine
**Vivaldi,** Calle della Madonnetta - San Polo 1457 ☎ 5289482
Family setting - local cuisine

## PUBS & PIANOBAR

**Antico Martini e Martini Scala**
Restaurant with piano bar
Campo San Fantin, 1983
☎ 5224121

**Linea d'ombra**
Restaurant with live music
Punta della Dogana - Zattere 12
☎ 5285259

**Le Bistrot de Venise**
Restaurant with cabaret, music and poetry
Calle dei Fabbri - San Marco 4685
☎ 5236651

**Il Paradiso Perduto**
Restaurant with music
Cannaregio, 2540
☎ 750581

**Devil's Forest pub**
Original music
Campo San Bartolomeo - Rialto
☎ 5236651

**The Fiddler's Elbow Irish Pub**
Cannaregio, 3847
☎ 5239930

## THEATERS AND CINEMAS

**La Fenice,** S. Fantin 2549
☎ 5210161
**Goldoni,** Calle Goldoni
☎ 5205422
**Del Ridotto,** Calle Vallaresso
☎ 5222939
**A l'Avogaria,** Dorsoduro 1617
☎ 5206130
**Fondamenta Nuove,** Cannaregio
5013 ☎ 5224498

**Accademia,** Dorsoduro 1019
☎ 5287706
**Centrale,** S. Marco 1659
☎ 5228201
**Olimpia,** S. Marco 1094
☎ 5205439
**Ritz,** S. Marco 617
☎ 5204429

## CASINOS

**Casinò Municipale di Venezia**
Palazzo Vendramin Calergi,
Cannaregio - San Marcuola
(in winter)
☎ 5297111

## DISCOTHEQUES

**Club el Souk**
Accademia 1056/a
☎ 5200371

# INDEX